Alexander Balloch Grosart, Herbert Palmer

**Lord Bacon**

Alexander Balloch Grosart, Herbert Palmer

**Lord Bacon**

ISBN/EAN: 9783337165819

Printed in Europe, USA, Canada, Australia, Japan

Cover: Foto ©Lupo / pixelio.de

More available books at **www.hansebooks.com**

# LORD BACON

*NOT THE AUTHOR OF*

## "THE CHRISTIAN PARADOXES:"

BEING A REPRINT OF

"𝔐𝔢𝔪𝔬𝔯𝔦𝔞𝔩𝔰 𝔬𝔣 𝔊𝔬𝔡𝔩𝔦𝔫𝔢𝔰𝔰 𝔞𝔫𝔡 𝔆𝔥𝔯𝔦𝔰𝔱𝔦𝔞𝔫𝔦𝔱𝔶,"

BY

# HERBERT PALMER, B.D.

WITH

*INTRODUCTION, MEMOIR, AND NOTES,*

BY THE

REV. ALEXANDER B. GROSART,

(COR. MEMB. SOC. ANTIQ. OF SCOT.)
KINROSS.

> "Out of the new fieldes, as men saith,
> Cometh all this new corn fro' year to year;
> And out of old bookes, in good faith,
> Cometh all this new science that men lere."
>
> — CHAUCER.

PRINTED FOR PRIVATE CIRCULATION.
1865.

To

## James Spedding Esq.,

*Editor*,

*in association with*

## R. L. Ellis Esq., and Douglas D. Heath Esq.,

*of*

*The Edition* facile princeps

*of*

## The Works of Bacon,

I offer

*This confirmation of his suspicion concerning the Non-Baconian authorship of " The Christian Paradoxes."*

" 'Tis my venture
On your retentive wisdom."—BEN JONSON.

*With much esteem and gratitude,*

ALEXANDER B. GROSART.

# PREFATORY NOTE.

IN "Introduction" I have given account of the remarkable little discovery that it has fallen to me to make, to wit, the non-Baconian, and actual, authorship of "The Christian Paradoxes." I briefly describe the different editions. Thereafter will be found illustrations of the evil influence against Bacon of his supposed authorship of these "Paradoxes," as misunderstood, more especially in France and Germany: and also of how the real authorship sweeps away the abounding guess-work as to their meaning and design. In a "Memoir" of Herbert Palmer, I have brought together, from all accessible sources, such facts and memorials as remain. In Appendix A there is given a *verbatim et literatim et punctatim* reprint of the surreptitious anonymous edition of the "Paradoxes," 1645; and in B the various readings as they appeared in "The Remaines," under the name of Bacon, 1648. Throughout the "Memorials" otherwise we have altered only the punctuation, and lessened the capitals and italics. We have adhered to the orthography with the exception of "then" for "than," which bothers a reader.* In Appendix C is a list of Palmer's other books and tractates; and I would invite attention to the angry notice by MILTON of a reference to his "Doctrine and Discipline of Divorce" made in the Fast-Sermon, the "Glasse of Providence," which is No. 3 in this List. A few Notes are added at close of the volume. In delivering this private reprint, which is limited to 100 copies large paper, and 150 small, I have to thank the authorities at the British Museum; Williams' Library; the Bodleian, Oxford; Charles H. Cooper, Esq., Cambridge; Joshua Wilson, Esq., Nevil Park, Tunbridge Wells; the Rev. David Y. Storrar, Penruddock, Penrith; and the Rev. John Hall of Bosmere Lodge, London, for assistance in the prosecution of my researches, most kindly rendered.

A. B. G.

FIRST MANSE,
KINROSS, *November* 1, 1864.

---

\* The reader will understand that in every case where "*than*" occurs as we would use it, it is in the original spelled "*then*." This is the only departure from Palmer's orthography; and, by keeping it in mind, there will be no difficulty to those who may use the little book for philological purposes—*e.g.*, Mr Furnival, of the "Philological Society," complains to me of even this single change.

# CONTENTS.

|  | PAGE |
|---|---|
| INTRODUCTION, | 1 |
| MEMOIR, | 25 |
| MEMORIALS— | |
|     Part I., | 49 |
|     Part II., | 73 |
|     Part III., | 97 |
| APPENDIX A— | |
|     Surreptitious Edition of "The Paradoxes," | 113 |
| APPENDIX B— | |
|     Various Readings from "The Remaines," | 117 |
| APPENDIX C— | |
|     Other Writings of Palmer, | 120 |
| APPENDIX D— | |
|     Ralph Venning's "Paradoxes," | 123 |
| NOTES, | 125 |

# PART I.

## INTRODUCTION.

THE little volume now reprinted is searching and suggestive, and has intrinsic weight and worth. It was highly prized by our Forefathers at a time when what are now our classics were being given to the world. It has gone out of sight much as the treasure-trove gold pieces that turn up occasionally in these days: purest "red gold," but out o' date. Our Memoir, it is believed, will satisfy that HERBERT PALMER was no common man, and verify the question of Sir Thomas Browne, "whether the best men be known, or whether there be not more remarkable persons forgot than any that stand remembered in the known account of time?"*

But probably the main interest and value of these "Memorials" is extrinsic, as enabling us finally to determine the non-Baconian authorship of "The Paradoxes," which for upwards of two centuries have been ascribed to Lord Bacon. As a literary fact, our little discovery has its own importance; and in view of the use that has been made of these striking aphorisms misunderstood, against Bacon, most will say, *Homo sum, Baconii nihil à me alienum puto*.

The following is the history of that portion of the "Memorials" in which our long-delayed discovery lies.

* Works, by Wilkin, vol. iii., page 492, (edn. by Pickering.)

Among the Thomason "Tracts" in the British Museum, there is what may be called a surreptitious edition of "The Paradoxes." The title-page runs:—

The
CHARACTER
of
*A Believing Christian.*
Set forth in *Paradoxes*, and
seeming *Contradictions.*
Imprimatur
JOSEPH CARYL.
London:
Printed for Richard Wodenothe, at
the Star, under *Peter's* Church in *Cornhill.*
1645.

It is a small 8vo, and, including title-page, makes 12 pages. On the title, with his usual exactness, Thomason has written "July 24," which denotes the day of publication. We give in Appendix A. a *verbatim* reprint of this first edition, by which it will be seen that it has no division into sections or other heads. It does not appear who prepared and published this anonymous version.*

I have called it a *surreptitious* edition of "The Paradoxes," because it was unauthorised by the author, as will appear from his vexed references in his "Epistle to the Christian Reader," when, under date "July 25"—*the very next day after the surreptitious edition*—he himself issued them. "I meant thee," he says, "somewhat more: but whilst (in the midst of many employments) I was getting it ready, *a strange hand was*

---

\* I owe my knowledge of this tract to the kindness of the editor of *Notes and Queries*, in his foot-note to my communication announcing the discovery, Sept. 17, 1864.

*like to have robbed me of the greatest part of this, by putting to the Presse (unknown to me) an imperfect copy of the Paradoxes.* This made me hasten to tender a *true one*, and to content myself for the present with the addition of the other lesser pieces which here accompany them." This "Epistle" is signed "Thine and the Churches servant together, Herbert Palmer," and is prefixed to Part II. of the "Memorials"—this second part being added to a new edition of Part I., which had been originally published in 1644, " December 13." The title-page corresponds precisely with that of all the subsequent editions that I have seen, and bears upon it the distinct announcement, among the other contents, " The Character of a Christian in Paradoxes and seeming Contradictions." By comparing Palmer's own text with that of the anonymous tractate, it will be seen that not without ground did he describe *it* as "imperfect." It will be observed, that the "true copy" arranged the aphorisms under eighty-five heads. Our reprint is *verbatim* from the "fifth edition, corrected," (1655) the corrections of the earlier editions, from 1645 to 1655, consisting apparently of almost verbal changes only—none whatever in " The Paradoxes." All the editions of the completed "Memorials," from first to last, bore the name of *Herbert Palmer* on the title-page, as well as the above separate note of "The Paradoxes," as forming a portion of the volume.

The earliest use of these aphorisms that I have found, is by John Saltmarsh in support of his (so-called) anti-Nomianism in his " Free Grace ; or, The Flowings of Christ's Blood freely to Sinners," &c. The *first* edition of this little book was also published in 1645. The "second and fifth editions corrected" are before me. They bear date 1646 and 1648 respectively; and in the Appendix, which is entitled, "Some truths of Free Grace sparkling in former Writers, and in some famous approved men of our times, in testimony to what is in this Discourse in part asserted, and in these times, by others, assertors of Free Grace," we have the following :—

"*God is never an enemy to his though sinning.*"—Mr Herbert Palmer in his Character of a Christian in Paradox, &c., p. 10.

"He believes the God that hates all sin, to be reconciled to himself, though sinning continually, and never making nor being able to make him satisfaction." [Cf. No. 10.]

"*We are justified though ungodly,*" p. 11.

"He believes the most just God, &c. to have justified himself, though a most ungodly sinner." [Cf. No. 11.]

"*We are not saved by anything we do,*" p. 58.

"He knows he shall not be saved by his works, and yet doth all the good works he can." [Cf. No. 58.]

"*A believer sins not,*" p. 68.

"He cannot sin, yet he can do nothing without sin." [Cf. No. 68.]

"*A believer believes against hope,*" p. 74.

"He believes like Abraham in hope against hope. [Cf. No. 74.]

"*God freely pardons,*" p. 12.

"He believes himself freely pardoned." [Cf. No. 12.]

"*Believers are pure in God's sight,*" p. 13.

"He believes himself to be precious in God's sight." [Cf. No. 13.]*

Having thus given an account of the "imperfect" and "true" editions of "The Paradoxes," it is necessary to correct an inadvertence of Mr Spedding's, from which it might seem that there had been an edition published in 1643, and bearing Bacon's name on the title page. Mr Spedding's words are :—"*The Character of a Believing Christian in Paradoxes and Seeming Contradictions,* is said to have appeared first in 1643 as a separate pamphlet, under Bacon's

* Pp. 214, 215, in both editions.

name."\* His authority is Rémusat. at p. 150, note. But on turning to Rémusat it is found that Mr Spedding has misread the date, overlooked a statement about the "three years" that elapsed between the pamphlet of 1645 and "The Remains" of 1648, and erred in supposing that Rémusat described the tractate of 1645 as bearing Bacon's name. Here is the note in full, of which more anon:
—"The Characters of a believing Christian in Paradoxes and seeming Contradictions; Works, t. ii., p. 494. Cet écrit fut publié pour la première fois en 1645, et inséré trois ans après dans les *Bacon's Remains*, in 4°, 1648. Or, tout n'est pas tenu pour authentique dans ce recueil. Rawley et Tenison publiant, l'un sa *Secunda Resuscitatio*, en 1658, l'autre son *Baconiana* en 1679, se sont plaints qu'on eût attribué à Bacon des ouvrages apocryphes, et ni l'un ni l'autre n'ont repris ni avoué les *Paradoxes;* que M. Montagu et M. Bouillet ne croient pas de Bacon. Mais il y a d'autres avis. Ritter penche à regarder l'ouvrage comme un essai de jeunesse, abandonné plus tard. (Montagu, t. vii., préf., p. xvi; Bouillet, t. i., p. 547, et t. ii., p. xxiii; Ritter, *Gesch. der Phil.*, t. x., p. 318.")†

Having communicated with Mr Spedding, he has kindly informed me that M. Rémusat was his only authority, and that consequently his statements based thereupon are oversights—which no one will be reluctant to pardon who knows how provokingly such slips happen, especially in so large an undertaking as that of Mr Spedding's Bacon.

The "imperfect copy" of "July 24, 1645," therefore, was the *first* edition of "The Paradoxes," and *it* is *anony-*

\* Works of Bacon, vii., p. 289.
† Bacon: sa Vie, son Temps, sa Philosophie, et son influence jusqu'à nos jours, par Charles de Rémusat. Paris, 1858, p. 150. One of the most thoughtful interpreters of Bacon, more than worthy of all Mr Spedding's praise.

*mous.* The *first* "true copy" is Palmer's own in Part II. of his "Memorials," published on "July 25," 1645. *No edition whatever bore the name of Bacon*, until in 1648 "The Paradoxes" were included in his "Remains."* In Appendix B, the various readings of this edition are furnished, by which it will be seen that they are divided into XXXIV. "heads:" and that there are slight departures from equally the "imperfect" anonymous text, and the "true copy" of Palmer.

How "The Paradoxes" came to be thus included in "The Remains" of Bacon—a volume "to which," observes Mr Spedding, "nobody stands sponsor,"†—it is impossible to say. Judging from internal and external evidence, there seem to be other pieces in it that are most certainly not "genuine:" while all who have had occasion to examine our early literature, are aware that it was a common trick to issue "imperfect," "false," and "unauthorised" writings, under any recently deceased name that might be expected to "take." The Puritans, down to John Bunyan, were perpetually expostulating and protesting against such procedure. *Whatever the explanation, it is plain that " The Paradoxes" were* NOT *Bacon's;* and that the author, *Herbert Palmer*, did not claim his own when they appeared in "The Remaines" is accounted for by his death in the previous year, 1647. The little book continued to be re-issued in successive editions under his own name: while, "The Paradoxes" were not included again in the Works of Bacon, as we shall see, until a long period had elapsed,—1730. Bacon's own executors

---

\* The Remaines of the Right Hon. Francis Lord Verulam, Viscount of *St Albans*, sometimes Lord Chancellor of *England*. Being Essayes and severall Letters to severall great Personages, and other pieces of various and high concernment not heretofore published. A Table whereof for the Readers more ease is adjoyned. London, Printed by B. Alsop for *Laurence Chapman*, and are to be sold at his Shop near the Savoy in the Strand. 1648, 4°.

† As before, vol. vi., p. 594.

and editors tacitly excluded them. Mr Spedding remarks, "Rawley says nothing of it: and as he can hardly be supposed to have overlooked it in the collection, his silence must be understood as equivalent to a statement that it was one of the many "pamphlets put forth under his lordship's name," which "are not to be owned for his."\* Tenison says nothing about it. No traces of it, or of any part of it, or of anything at all resembling it, are to be found among the innumerable Baconian manuscripts, fair and foul,—fragments, rough notes, discarded beginnings, loose leaves,—which may still be seen at Lambeth, in the British Museum, and other repositories.†

After "The Remaines" of 1648 the first edition of the "Works" of Bacon which included "The Paradoxes" was Blackburn's, 1730; from a note in which it would appear that Archbishop Sancroft "revised," or, as Blackburn puts it, gave them "a careful review;" the meaning of which is explained to be, that he had "compared" it "with the other copy, printed Lond. anno 1645;" and by which again must be understood the surreptitious and anonymous edition described by us. Ever since Blackburn's edition of the "Works," "The Paradoxes" have been included therein, with less or more of suspicion. Basil Montagu, Esq.—whose judgment, however, was not at all equal to his industry—has given a summary of the evidence on either side,‡ which it is curious to read in the light of our discovery, a discovery that might have been made any time during these two centuries and upwards.§

So recently as a couple of months ago, in a very admir-

\* Resuscitatio, at the end.     † As before, vii., p. 289.
‡ Works of Bacon, vol. vii., pp. xxvi–xl.

§ Let it be kept in mind to add to the uniqueness of the continued oversight, that from 1645 to 1708, the "Memorials" passed through *thirteen* distinct editions. The 10th, 1670, is said to be "enlarged;" but this refers to a little Memoir abridged from Clarke, [pp. 18, unpaged.] It

able volume of " Selections " from the Works of Bacon, in the " Wisdom of our Fathers," having the imprint of the " Religious Tract Society," the " Paradoxes " are given in full, and prefixed is this note :—" The authenticity of this tract has been called in question, but without sufficient reason. The internal evidence on its behalf is strong ; and parallel passages may be found in his acknowledged works, which appear to be either the germs or the developed forms of many of these striking antitheses."\* How these "aphorisms" could be " the *developed* forms," and at the same time "*germs*," would need explanation. But after our account, "internal evidence" here, as in other cases, goes for nothing.

So much for the correction of a two-century-old literary error, if not fraud.

T may not be without advantage next to shew how " The Paradoxes" have been interpreted, and especially how, as *misunderstood*, they have been employed against Bacon. Those who do me the honour to read the little Memoir of Herbert Palmer, which follows this, will be satisfied that these " Paradoxes" were the production of a profoundly religious and believing man. Hence, especially in the face of previous misinterpretations of their spirit, and in ignorance of the real author, it argued considerable acumen and resolution on the part of Mr Spedding to write of them as he did. We may here give his judgment :—

---

closes thus : "And thus he lived, and so he dyed ; and now he's dead, his works do live." The 11th edition was published, Part III. in 1671, Part II. in 1673, Part I. in 1681, including the others. Our examination of the different editions shews no changes in " The Paradoxes ;" so that our text (1655) represents the " true copy " given by Palmer himself. It is surprising that Sir Egerton Brydges did not anticipate our discovery. In his " Restituta " (iv. 366) he records the 5th edition, 1655, gives the "Contents," and also some of " The Paradoxes"!

\* Pp. 1, 2, and 13-20.

"In the opinions and sentiments which the work implies, there is nothing from which I should infer either that it was not Bacon's or that it was. It is the work of an orthodox Churchman of the early part of the 17th century, who, fully and unreservedly accepting, on the authority of revelation, the entire scheme of Christian theology, and believing that the province of faith is altogether distinct from that of reason, found a pleasure in bringing his spiritual loyalty into strong relief by confronting and numbering up the intellectual paradoxes which it involved. In these days of uncertain faith it has indeed been mistaken for sarcastic; but I can have no doubt whatever that it was written (whoever wrote it) in the true spirit of *credo quia impossible*, and not only in perfect sincerity, but also in profound security of conviction. One might as well suppose that the Athanasian Creed* was written in derision of the particular doctrine of the Trinity, as that this was written in derision of

---

\* We daresay Mr Spedding imagined that he was putting his case as strongly as possible in adducing the Athanasian Creed: and few will differ. But the " Passages from the Life of a Philosopher," (1864,) by Charles Babbage, Esq., supplies us with this marvellous criticism:—

"If I were to express my opinion of the Athanasian Creed merely from my experience of the motives and actions of mankind, I should say that it was written by a *clever*, but most unscrupulous person, *who did not believe one syllable of the doctrine*,—that he purposely asserted and reiterated propositions which contradict each other in terms, in order that in after and more enlightened times, he should not be supposed to have believed in the religion which he had, *from worldly motives*, adopted," (pp. 403, 404.) Indeed and indeed, Mr Babbage! "*clever*" applied to the author of the "Athanasian Creed"! It reminds us of a lady telling us the Falls of Niagara were "pretty." And Athanasius "*did not believe one syllable of the doctrine*," with History and Biography full of counter-evidence, that, while he cannot certainly be regarded as the writer of the Creed which bears his illustrious name, *it*, nevertheless, embodied his faith and often-expressed opinions. Who is the "*unscrupulous* person" is not far to seek, notwithstanding Note B in his Appendix, and our appreciation of a large-brained man. This and his "Miracles" chapter compell us to recall the saying of Apelles, "*Ne sutor ultra crepidam.*"

the doctrines of the Christian Church in general. As far as the opinions are concerned, therefore, it might well enough have been written by Bacon, for we know that he did earnestly believe, and continually insist upon the necessity of keeping the domains of Reason and Faith distinct."*

A century before Mr Spedding, a somewhat eccentric "clergyman" of the name of Green published "The Paradoxes," in a penny tract, as Bacon's: and the editor thus "prefaces" them with mingled caution and spiritual discernment:—

"In order to prevent a misconstruction of the following Paradoxes, it may be needful to inform the Reader, that, when rightly considered, they are no ways ludicrous, sarcastical, or profane, but solid, comfortable and godly truths taught by the Holy Ghost in the School of Experience, and well understood by those who are truly Christians.

"I do not say that every 'babe' in Christ can understand them all; but this I think I may venture to affirm, he that understands none of them hath not yet learned his A B C in the School of Christ.

"But if any should ask of me why I choose to publish his Lordship's Paradoxes rather than any other, I answer, 1st, Because though very comprehensive, yet they are but short, and may therefore be easily purchased by the poorer sort of Christians. 2dly, That the Minute Philosophers and ignoble Gentlemen of our day might here be taught that a fine gentleman, a sound scholar, and a great philosopher may be a Christian, since we find not only a Paul, a Justin Martyr, &c., but even in our own nation so good a Philosopher as any, Lord Bacon, espousing and confessing the Christian verity.

"In a word, Reader, if thou understand those few Paradoxes, bless God for them; if thou understandest them not, thou mayest, like the Eunuch, call in some Philip to thy assistance: but above all permit me to advise thee to ask of

* As before, vii., p. 290.

the Father of Lights, who giveth wisdom liberally and upbraideth not. I am for Christ's sake
"Thy friend and servant,
"J. GREEN."*

Scarcely anything of the point of the rebuke of the "Minute Philosophers" is lost by substituting the name of Herbert Palmer for that of Bacon. We find very much what we bring to anything, be it landscape or book : and the true explanation of the misunderstanding and mis-estimate of "The Paradoxes," as designed to be "sarcastical," is to be found in the wish to have them so, the "wish being father of the thought." The blundering reading of them is chiefly traceable to the French sceptical writers, as Bayle, Condillac, Cabanis, Lasalle, with whom may be classed David Mallet. These claim Bacon as an "atheist," than which anything more monstrous is inconceivable. I am not concerned to vindicate Bacon from the charge and claim ; but I am glad to think that our discovery enables us to remove "The Paradoxes" from Infidelity, and from those who on the strength (or weakness) of their interpretation (or perversion) have sought to atheize England's Second Thinker. The most cursory perusal of the books of the above names, reveals "The Paradoxes" as the quiver whence the keenest shafts are fetched to smite the "Religion" of Bacon. Joseph de Maistre, also,

* "Characteristics of a believing Christian in Paradoxes, and seeming Contradictions, by Francis Bacon, Baron of Verulam, Vicount [*sic*] of St Albans, and Lord High Chancellor of England. With a Preface by a Clergyman. The Second Edition. London : Printed in the year 1758, (Price one penny,) 8vo." A copy is preserved in the British Museum, where are also various books and pamphlets by Green, who seems to have fallen into a strangely chequered life. He divides the Paradoxes into thirty-two. Montagu quotes the above Preface from a 3d edition, 1762 ; but makes his signature F., which is a mistake, as his name was John Green "of Thurnscoe," &c.

in his amazing (or amusing) farrago, " Examen de la Philosophie de Bacon, où l'on traite différentes Questions de la Philosophie rationnelle," (Paris, 2 vols. 1836,) in which, from a Roman Catholic stand-point, he refuses to regard our illustrious Philosopher as other than a dis-Believer and Infidel and " Mocker,"— stumbles at the same " stone." His fieryest darts are quenched by our simple disproof of the long alleged authorship of " The Paradoxes."

It must not be forgotten that while France has thus slandered and dishonoured Bacon, she has also furnished a most thorough and exhaustive treatise on his "genuine " Christianhood—viz., the " Christianisme de Bacon " of Emery; and more recently we have the " Précis de la Philosophie de Bacon " of De Luc.

But to return: M. Rémusat has unquestionably laid the disciples and admirers of Bacon under a deep debt of gratitude for his masterly and subtle book already noticed: nor may we pass over the ponderous sciomachy of the German Ritter. But inasmuch as underlying all M. Rémusat's suspicions of the Christian character of Bacon, and intensifying the vulgar audacities and impertinences of Ritter's unmeasured assault, there is a tacit recollection of " The Paradoxes" *misunderstood*, I deem it right to proclaim the fact, and in the measure of it empty it of its force for evil. I pause upon each.

1. *Dr Heinrich Ritter:* In his " Geschichte der Phil.," (vol. x.,) with its triple title, " History of Philosophy," "History of Christian Philosophy," and " History of Modern Philosophy," (Perthes, Hamburg 1851,) we have a most depreciatory and, indeed, pestiferous exposition of Bacon's character. As this elaborate work has its own merits, spite of its abounding prejudices and ignorances, and as it has not been translated, I give a specimen or two to shew incidentally the evil effect of the wrong authorship of " The Para-

doxes," and of consequent blundering over them. At page 318, we read,—" There can be no doubt about the duplicity and weakness of the character of Bacon. In a letter to Thomas Bodley, he confesses the great mistake of his life, that, though drawn by inward inclination to the sciences, he devoted himself to the employments of public life, whilst his heart was not there. It is sad to remark that he should thus have made confession to a friend of this his unfaithfulness to his destined sphere, and yet should not have found in himself the strength to apply the remedy. It was a confession rather of the lip than of the heart. Avarice and vanity were the ruling passions of his nature; and that, too, of a man whose lips were fraught with the precepts of wisdom, whilst he was a drudge to the world's follies, and allowed himself to be borne on by them to deeds the most criminal, and words the most base. So vain were his thoughts, that he felt not the odiousness of his life. His spirit was naturally inclined to mildness, and yet he permitted himself to be made an instrument in measures the most severe; and, with no attachment to persons or his people, he seeks only his own glory, and seeks it in things the most worthless. There was no trusting to his words, even when he seemed to speak in the name of science. He professes love to the Church of England, and to the Christian religion; BUT HIS LOVE TO CHRISTIANITY *becomes very doubtful when we read his Christian* 'PARADOXES.'" There it is. The purblind philosopher knocks his muddled head against "The Paradoxes." To this a foot-note is appended: " The Christian Paradoxes appeared after his death, 1645. They have it for their object to exhibit the seeming contradictions of the Christian faith in the sharpest and broadest form. It cannot be supposed that he meant to vanquish these ill-digested contradictions, *accumulated on purpose*, with that *Credo quia absurdum est* of the 'De Augm. Scient.,'

(ix. 1, p. 263.) The genuineness of 'The Paradoxes' has been called in question, *but apparently without just grounds.*'" Mark the malignity of the italicised words, "*accumulated on purpose.*" Mark how jauntily, also, the questioning of the Baconian authorship is dismissed, "*apparently without just grounds.*" A theory was to be supported, and "The Paradoxes" were indispensable to it. He resumes and continues: "It may, indeed, be so far alleged in his favour, that this little treatise may have been only the crude utterances or effusion of a scepticism which he afterwards suppressed; because, otherwise, we must assume him to have been a consummate hypocrite, and that, too, when he had no end to serve by it, in the very plays of his intellect, or his confiding utterances to his friends—*e.g.*, his Confession of his Faith, his forms of Prayer, his translations of the Psalms."

In the above foot-note, Ritter refers to Bacon's "*Credo quia absurdum est,*"—"I believe because it is hard of belief." And onward (p. 320) he tells us that it was a sentiment of Bacon's, "that we ought to subject our reason to faith; and that the more distasteful and hard of belief anything appears to us, the more ought we to believe it,"—a densely stupid caricature of Bacon's teaching, which really is, that we ought to believe, ought to accept the impossible, (so-called,) when for that alleged impossible thing *we have the authority of God's revealed Word.* Faith in *it* overleaps the impossible —TRUSTS GOD. To any but a mind of the Ritter stamp, this lies on the very surface of the passage quoted, which may be thus rendered:—"Therefore the more difficult and hard of belief any *Divine mystery* is, the more honour do we render to God in believing it, and the greater is the victory of our faith. It is indeed a nobler thing to believe than to know as we know now," &c. After this how shall we characterise the foot-note on p. 318:—"*It cannot be believed* that

Bacon, in exhibiting so broadly as in 'The Paradoxes' the seeming contradictions of the Christian faith, should have done so *that he might leave room for the operation of his own principle*, that the harder of belief anything revealed to us by God is, the more ought we to believe it?" Why not? we naturally ask. Of course Bacon did not write "The Paradoxes" at all; but very base is this attempt to set aside the play and application of "his own principle" while assuming and arguing that he was their author.

The opening sentences of our extract shew a profound and contemptible misapprehension, alike of Bacon's touching words and of his acts. But Mr Hepworth Dixon has sufficiently and chivalrously, and with surpassing eloquence and success, vindicated him herein; and I have only to do with Ritter in so far as his mistakes of fact and of inference are referable to "The Paradoxes." In disproving their Baconian authorship, Ritter's charges and flippancies disappear.

2. *M. Charles de Rémusat.* It is not very creditable that while the infinitely inferior, though of its kind able "F. Bacon ... Die Realphilosophie und ihr Zeitalter" of Kuno Fischer (1856) has been translated into English, the suggestive and invaluable treatise of M. Rémusat still lies unrendered. We must hold that M. Rémusat has not given sufficient weight to the innumerable expressions of Bacon's own religious opinions and belief, more especially we have to lament that he has overlooked his more recondite and unstudied, incidental, almost accidental, utterances, in private "Letters," and the like. We do not see how any one can bring these together, and study them, as may be readily done in the "Christianisme de Bacon" of Emery, or, better still, in the "Selections" of "The Religious Tract Society," already referred to, or in the work named below,*

* Thoughts on Holy Scripture. By Francis Bacon, Lord Chan-

without being struck with the devout and reverential attitude habitual to Bacon towards the Christian Revelation. What would we not give for the like personal utterances by William Shakespeare! But I am bound to submit M. Rémusat's observations, all the more that, perhaps, unconsciously to himself, the "Paradoxes" tinge his whole estimate of the religious character of Bacon. At p. 148 onward, we read :—" We cannot speak of his soul without asking what were his religious opinions? This is a point which needs some clearing up. We have not said anything concerning it, and it does not appear that those, his religious opinions, played an important part in his life. No one doubts but that he respected, as a precious trust, the order established in the Church. He would have devised Erastianism, if such had been necessary, in company with Archbishop Parker, primate under Elizabeth, a college friend of Cecil and Bacon. But we shall add that, if not in his sentiments, at least in his creed, he was Christian. Doubt has been expressed on this matter; his works do not abound in explicit and detailed declarations on the dogmas of his faith. It has even been made matter of reproach against him that he has written so much, and yet so little on religion. There is nothing that indicates in him a very decided tendency to piety. His contempt for scholastic authorities, his predilection for the positive sciences and experimental researches, the terrestrial character, if we may be permitted the expression, of his philosophy, the consequences which empirical learning has drawn from them, the homage which our eighteenth century rendered to him, the doubtful honour of having been taken by D'Alembert and Diderot as their masters,

cellor of England. Compiled by John G. Hall, Fort Plain, New York. With Preface by John Cairns, D.D., 1862. 1 vol., cr. 8vo. The whole of the "Paradoxes" are given in scattered extracts, and there are other non-"genuine" quotations; but it is an acceptable compilation.

might have caused reasonable doubt to be entertained concerning the nature or reality of his religious faith : we shall admit even that scepticism, or, to be more accurate, a kind of free-thinking, accused by the different churches as scepticism, has been known to be more extensively prevalent in the modern world than is believed, or at least than is avowed: and the protestations and reservations of an orthodox character made by great minds do not inspire us with a very great confidence." Then comes in the sinister and baleful influence of "The Paradoxes" *misunderstood*, and of the erroneous Baconian authorship :—" Part of the numerous passages in which Bacon has made the most favourable allusions to Christianity might be cast aside by painstaking critics who should call to mind what he has said about the suitable and proper use of dissimulation. It were possible to believe that it is nothing but convenient phrases, the common use of language, in one word, a mere orthodoxy of phraseology. Yet must we remark, that if, by deductions more or less specious, some of his views have been made to lend countenance and support to irreligion, irreligion has inspired none of his books : none of them which has had for its professed object the denial or even the unhinging of any religious dogma. One only of the treatises ascribed to him may, by a possibility, create doubts. There was published as a treatise of his, 19 years after his death, some pages on Christian belief; where 34 paragraphs are occupied with proving that the articles of belief have all the character of paradox and of contradiction : and the last, after having set over against the finite nature of man an infinite blessedness, concludes with these words,—' Glory be to God.' " There follows as a foot-note what has been given already, (page 5.) He then proceeds with a candour in fine contrast with the dogmatic shallowness and prejudgment of Ritter.

" At first the authenticity of this little work was not entirely established by individual proofs, and has been contested on very good grounds. There is observable in the treatise, indeed, a logical precision, an antithetic and pointed form, which is not very characteristic of the author's manner. In fine, whatever its origin may be, it is possible that this same treatise may be designed, whether as a simple exercise of intellect, or a comparison between the dogmas of faith and the dictates of common sense, which would not necessarily indicate his intention to sacrifice the one to the other, yea, might even be conceived with the quite opposite purpose. All these *sic et non* are not the declarations of a religious scepticism; and a highly respected Catholic theologian has even seen in the Paradoxes of Bacon a new proof in favour of his faith. It might be thus the result of an impartial and attentive examination. It is a very exact comparison and confronting with each other of the different parts of the Christian doctrine, from which he may have gone forth as humble, as faithful, as sincere, and profound, and heartfelt a Christian as he was before." Here a foot-note is added: " Without venturing to go that length, we would merely say that a treatise whose origin is doubtful, and also its meaning and object, cannot overcome, in our estimation, the authority of the numerous passages in which Bacon speaks in an orthodox manner. It would be too long to indicate these here: and we shall return to the subject when we come to study his philosophy." Then another footnote: " But nothing can authorise us in doubting the sincerity of his professions; and it appears to us, that without any of the inward fervour of a true Christian, Bacon was bound by the character of his mind to adhere, without opposition and without hesitation, to the faith of his country and of his government, even though we should discard the doubtful testimony of his secretary, William Rawley, who says that he faithfully practised the duties of religion, and that he died in its belief." What follows is exceedingly weighty, and with nice felicity worded; but it were out of place to go beyond what touches "The Paradoxes." Finally: To shew how little value "internal evidence" of "style," and the like has, even in the hands of an undoubted scholar, let us hear Dr Samuel Parr about "The Paradoxes." In a letter to his Biographer, E. H. Barker, Esq., he says, *inter alia :* "It is, however, well known that some of his fragments were not acknowledged by Dr Rawley to be genuine, though vouched to be authentic in an edition of the 'Remains of Lord Verulam,' printed in 1648, and though examined, corrected, and prepared for the press by Archbishop Sancroft, among the other unquestionable writings of Bacon. Among those fragments are the Character of a believing Christian, in paradoxes and seeming contradictions, compared with the copy printed, Lond. 1645. The paradoxes are thirty-four; but it is sufficient for my purpose to quote the 2d and 3d. After frequent and most attentive perusal, *I am convinced that these Fragments were written by Bacon*, and intended only for a trial of his skill in putting together propositions, which appear irreconcilable; and that we ought to be very wary in drawing from such a work any positive conclusions upon the real and settled faith of Lord Bacon. Bacon perhaps was sincere, when he said, 'I had rather believe all the fables in the Legend, and the Talmud, and the Alcoran, than that this universal frame is without a mind.' But to many parts of the Paradoxes we may apply his remark upon the fool who *said* in his heart, but did not *think*, 'There is no God.' He rather said these things for a trial of skill, as the fool talked by rote, than that he really believed them, or was persuaded of them." Similarly, in a letter to Mr C. Butler, published in Butler's "Reminiscences," (vol. ii., p. 233,) he says: "But now comes a real difficulty. What shall we say to the 'Character of a believing Christian in paradoxes and seeming contradictions?' Here I am quite at a loss to determine. If an ingenious man means to deride the belief of Christianity, could he have done it more effectually than in the work just now alluded to? Mr Hume would say, No. There is some uncertainty as to the authenticity of this little tract. I suspect that Bacon meant to try his strength, and then to return quietly to the habitual conviction of his mind, that Christianity is true."\* O "purblind Argus, all eyes and no sight!" But all this suspicion and misinference concerning Lord Bacon is swept away by the now proved non-Baconian authorship: while equally is this guess-work as to the real meaning and intention of "The Paradoxes" removed by a knowledge of who and what the actual author was.

IT only remains here briefly to notice certain other books and tractates of the class to which "The Paradoxes" belongs. Like the word "Marrow," which is found on at least a hundred old title-pages, (apart from what is known in Scotland as "The Marrow Controversy,") this of "Paradoxes" seems to have been a taking one in England and on the Continent. The "Paradoxa" of Cicero were early "Englyshed" by Robert Whittington, "Poet Laureat," (1540,) and by Thomas Newton, "Physician, Poet, Divine, and Schoolmaster," and by others.

Dr Donne, besides his "ΒΙΑΘΑΝΑΤΟΣ: a Declaration of that *Paradoxe* or Thesis, that Selfe-Homicide is not so naturally Sinne that it may never be otherwise," (1644,) had previously entitled one of his most original, and by far too little known books, "Juvenilia: or, *Paradoxes* and Problems," (1633 and 1652.)

The "Poems" of Henry King, Bishop of Chichester, were originally published anonymously as " Poems, Elegies, *Para-*

---

\* Quoted in Montagu's Bacon, as before, vii., pp. xxvi.–xxviii.

*doxes*, and Sonnets," (1657,) and when the unsold copies in the hands of an unprincipled bookseller were re-issued, it was as "Ben Jonson's Poems, Elegies, *Paradoxes*, and Sonnets," (1700.) Somewhat before this, Henry Peacham—whose initials only appear in the title-page, and hence have been confounded with those of Herbert Palmer—furnishes us with "*Paradox* in praise of a Dunse in Sweetyman's, by H. P." (1642.) But by far the most remarkable volume of this class—and it is a very remarkable one—is the following: "Orthodox *Paradoxes*, Theoreticall and Experimentall, or a Believer clearing truth by *Seeming Contradictions*. With an Appendix called the Triumph of Assurance. By Ralph Venning of Immanuell Colledge in Cambridge." Our copy is "the third edition, with some marginall additions," 1650. The *first* seems to have been published in 1647. The secondary title would suggest knowledge of Palmer's—but an examination shews no intended sarcasm under "Orthodox." The "Paradoxes" are as boldly stated: but are worked out and amplified with great ingenuity and practical usefulness.*

Besides these, Watt, in his "Bibliotheca Britannica," and other bibliographers, register a number of books and tractates more or less resembling, by Continental divines and men of science—as Brandolinus and Husman, Malvezzi and Malgnes, Von Helmont and Freitag, Clave and Granger, Hoornbeeck and Salle, Morellet and Sandius, and Paracelsus, and others early and comparatively recent. The "wits" of Queen Anne's reign also found "*Paradox*" a word to 'conjure' with: and Judge Long, in Jamaica, seems to have used it to tighten the fetters of the negro. Professor De Morgan, in our day, is delighting the readers of the *Athenæum* with the treasures of his out-of-the-way mathematical reading, under the caption, "A Budget of *Paradoxes*."

* For further details see Appendix D.

As not the least curious thing in the history of these "Paradoxes," I give the title-page and contents of a trans-Atlantic volume, which has created for its author considerable fame. They will speak for themselves :—

CHRISTIAN PARADOXES.

By

N. M. Crawford, D.D.,

President of Mercer University, Penfield, Georgia.

Nashville:

South-Western Publishing House,

Graves, Marks, & Co.

New York:

Sheldon, Blakeman, & Co.,

1858.

(Title-Page; "Invocation," "Dedication," "Preface,"

pp. vi. and 444.)

CONTENTS:

Chapter
- I. Man is a Sinner.
- II. The Sinner is alive and yet dead.
- III. The Change. The Sinner a Child of Wrath, becomes a Christian, a Child of God.
- IV. The Christian is dead and yet alive.
- V. The Christian is buried and yet has risen again.
- VI. All that the Christian can do will not procure Salvation, yet he should work as if Salvation depended upon each one of his Works.
- VII. The Christian receives Eternal Life as a Free Gift from God, and yet is rewarded by God according to his Deeds.
- VIII. The Christian is justified and yet forgiven.

## Introduction.

Chapter
- IX. The Christian is justified by Faith without the Deeds of the Law, and yet is justified by Works.
- X. The Invitations of the Gospel are general and unlimited, while the Redemption and Salvation provided in the Gospel are particular and definite.
- XI. The Christian is warned of Danger, yet his Salvation is secure.
- XII. The Christian is atoned for by a Priest, and yet is himself both a Priest and a Sacrifice.
- XIII. The Christian is always at War, and yet may enjoy constant Peace.
- XIV. The Christian knows not what to pray for, and yet does pray, and prevails in Prayer.
- XV. The Christian is weak, and yet strong. Unequal to the smallest Work, he is intrusted with the greatest.
- XVI. The Christian is poor, and yet rich.
- XVII. The Christian is despised, and yet honorable.
- XVIII. The Christian is unknown, and yet well known.
- XIX. The Christian is sorrowful, yet rejoicing.
- XX. The Christian is a Slave, and yet free.
- XXI. The Christian is fearful and yet bold.
- XXII. The Christian is loved, and yet afflicted.
- XXIII. The Occupation and Duties of the Christian are on Earth, his Citizenship is in Heaven.

There is nothing very memorable in this book : no grasping of that harmony which underlies, deeper far than all their "*seeming* contradictions," the successive Paradoxes,— no descending to the profound, divine calm that bears up the hugest surface-turmoil, as does the strong sea in its broad depths the agitation of its infinitude of waves,— no gleam of star, no moonëd glory illumining the vast-shadowed mysteries that lie folded in the "mystery of godliness, God manifest in the flesh." Nevertheless, after its own kind the book is a good one, abating its "strong yet weak" Americanisms. But how this minister

of the Gospel of Him who is "The Truth" could print that
"Invocation," and write his personally explanatory "Preface," and in not the most distant form anywhere acknowledge indebtedness to either Palmer or Bacon or Venning,
is another "Paradox" which we should like to have solved
by him or his critics.

And so I go on to tell the story of the life of HERBERT
PALMER. Turn the leaf: and with Quarles, "I wish thee
as much pleasure in the reading as I had in the writing."

# PART II.

## MEMOIR.

THOSE who are fortunate enough to possess the noble folio of SAMUEL CLARKE, "Pastor of St Bennet Fink, London,"—his "General Martyrologie," with its appendix-volume of the "Lives of Thirty-two English Divines" (1677, 3d edition) will find therein a full and loving Memoir of "Master Herbert Palmer, B.D.,"—so he is styled under the noticeable portrait; child-like face, large-eyes, thought-worn features,—by this twin-brother among our old Biographers, to Isaac Walton, and Thomas Fuller, and Clement Barksdale.

The Memoir partakes of its worthy author's excursiveness and unexpected digressions—provoking perchance to the mere searcher for dates, but thrice welcome to all who deem it good to escape now and then from the hurry and sensationalism of the present into the wood-like tranquillity and "large leisure" of the Past. To CLARKE I must refer the reader who wishes for minute details of fact together with many wise and witty, nor unseldom memory-haunting, "*improvements*" thereof: these given with that guileless lingering which reminds us that the saintly "Pastor" of those times was used to turn "the glass," and go on for another hour without complaint.

What I propose here is to follow up our introduction to the BOOK by giving a brief sketch of the Life of the MAN, embracing *memorabilia* gleaned from all available sources in scattered print and manuscript.

THE Palmers appear to have been a very ancient family in Kent. The father of our Worthy was Sir Thomas Palmer of Wingham in East Kent, about six miles from Canterbury. His mother was the eldest daughter of *Herbert* Pelham, Esq. of Crawley in Sussex : hence his Christian name. He was born in the family mansion of Wingham, and "was there baptized, March 29, 1601." Both father and mother were pre-eminently "godly" in its Bible and Puritan meaning. They are represented as watching over little Herbert with no common wistfulness and tenderness: and the old words in the old book concerning Jeremiah and John the Baptist are applied to him, "*sanctified from the womb.*" When he was "about the age of four or five years he would cry to go to his lady-mother that 'he might hear somewhat of God.'"* Neither, observes his Biographer, "did these and such-like expressions of affection to good things soon vanish away, (as childish apprehensions use to do,) but continued and increased, according as his years and the use of reason increased. Hence was it, that even from a child, being asked at any time what course of life he best liked to follow, whether to be a lawyer, a courtier, a country gentleman, &c., he would still answer, that he would be a minister of Jesus Christ." "From which," continues Clarke, "while some of his friends, for trial sake, would seem to dissuade him as being too mean an employment for a gentleman, telling him that ministers are hated, despised, and accounted as the off-scouring of the world, &c., he would reply, 'It was no matter for that ; for if the world hated him, yet God

* Clarke, *above*, pp. 183, 184.

would love him.'"* As was to be expected, "he was early acquainted with the Book of God, which he much delighted in, and read with great affection—insomuch that while he was but a child, little more than five years old, he wept in reading the story of Joseph, and took much pleasure in learning of chapters by heart."† One recalls another little boy in the light of this, Master Timothy couched at the knee of "grandmother Lois and mother Eunice," (2 Tim. i. 5.) It was out of the grave, pious child-life of this sort grew up the Sir John Eliots, and Pyms, and Hampdens, and Oliver Cromwells, who gave its profound religiousness to the great after-movement in which, in common with them, Master Herbert was destined to play his part.

Precocious in " grace," he was not less so in natural gifts. " He had excellent natural parts, both intellectual and moral : which as they were soon capable of being employed, so they were soon set on work ; his parents' vigilancy being such that they suffered no time to be neglected."‡ By some happy accident he acquired French very soon. On this and its advantages his Biographer already cited must be allowed to speak : " He learned," says he, " the French tongue almost as soon as he could speak English ; even so soon as that he hath often affirmed he did not remember his learning of it. And he did afterwards attain so great exactness of speaking and preaching in that language, together with a perfect knowledge of the state and affairs of that kingdom, especially of the Protestant Church amongst them, that he was often, by strangers, thought to be a native Frenchman ; and did not doubt but to entertain discourse with any person of that nation for some hours together in their own language concerning the affairs of that kingdom, who should not be able by his discourse to distinguish him from a native French-

* Clarke, above, p. 184.　　† Ibid., p. 184.　　‡ Ibid.

man, but judge him to be born and bred in France; so well was he furnished with an exact knowledge both of the propriety and due pronunciation of that language, and of the persons, places, and affairs of that kingdom, and the Churches therein: a thing not often seen in one who had never been out of England."*

Of his school-days altogether this is the "testimony": "When he learned the Latin tongue, with such other parts of learning as younger years are usually employed in at school, his diligence and proficiency therein was such as produced both commendation and admiration, [= wonder.] And while others at vacant hours were following their sports and recreations, he was constantly observed to be reading studiously by himself, taking as much pleasure in good employment as others in sports: and counting that the best passe-time wherein the time was best passed."† Very good pun, ancient "Pastor of St Bennet Fink:" but our little Puritan had been at "*good employment*" also if he had joined in the "*sports*," oftener lifted his wise small face from his books, and chased the butterflies on the meadows, or tossed his curls on the breezy wolds. All too soon was Master Herbert worn and pallid: and so mournfully early went away.

He proceeded to Cambridge, and "about the year 1615" —that is, in his fourteenth or fifteenth year—was admitted a Fellow-Commoner in St John's College, "where he continued his former diligence, as well in the exercise of religion as the improvement of his learning; both in his private study and in the performance of exercises in the University and College, notwithstanding the exemption to which Fellow-Commoners in Colleges are ready to plead from the performance of them."‡ "After that," Clarke informs us—and I have found nearly all his statements

* Clarke, *above*, p. 184.  † Ibid.  ‡ Ibid., p. 185.

verified by other authorities consulted, " he had there taken the degree of Master of Arts about the year 1622; he was in the year 1623 constituted Fellow of Queen's College; where, although he was a gentleman that, beside his fellowship, had an estate of his own, and so had the less need in point of maintenance to take that trouble of pupils upon him: yet—not satisfying himself to take a place upon him without performing the office thereunto belonging—he took many pupils, of whom he was more than ordinarily careful, being very diligent both in praying with them in his chamber and instructing them in the grounds of religion; as also keeping them to their studies, and the performance of disputations and other exercises of learning privately in his chamber, beside the more public exercises required of them by the College, to the great benefit of those that were his pupils."* Most laudable fidelity, most winsome humbleness surely: and yet the Royalist Cole has nothing for it all but the angry nickname phrase, "where he was pupil-monger."† While he was Fellow of Queen's College, " about the year 1624, he was solemnly ordained to the work of the ministry, whereunto from a child he had addicted himself." ‡ About the year 1626 he was " called to the public exercise" of his ministry as a "*Lecturer* in the city of Canterbury." The occasion and circumstances of this call—a home-visit and accidental Sermon—are told in his own full, quaint way by Clarke, in which tribute is paid to Master Delme, " a godly, faithful,

* Clarke, as before, p. 185.
† Cole MSS. in the British Museum: addit. MS., 5808, pp. 152-155. The extraordinary industry of William Cole, the Antiquary of Cambridge is above praise, but his spirit is worse than Anthony a-Wood's. His facts and data are valuable: his judgment perverse; his opinions worthless. He is specially rabid against all who sided not with the king in everything; and so against Palmer.
‡ Clarke, as before, p. 185.

prudent and laborious minister of the French Church in Canterbury," the fragrance of whose memory has not yet exhaled in the place. * Suffice it to say, that after another Sermon on a week-day Lecture, "the most godly and best affected in the city" being "more and more taken with him, expressed great 'desires of enjoying his ministry amongst them, if it might be obtained." "Whereupon Master Delme, with divers others of the most considerable gentlemen and citizens, having earnestly sought direction from God in a matter of such concernment, did seriously advise about it; and being first assured of the concurrent desires of many others, did by letters and messages to Cambridge signify to him the desire of the godly in that city that he would undertake to preach a Lecture amongst them." The issue was that the "invitation, after mature deliberation," and with no small self-sacrifice, was accepted. "Whereupon a licence being obtained for him from George Abbot, then Archbishop of Canterbury, authorising him to preach a Lecture on the Lord's-day, in the afternoon, at *Alphage* Church," in Canterbury, he "left his fellowship in the University and undertook this work." † So Clarke: but in regard to the fellowship Cole corrects him thus: "This is a mistake as may be seen from y$^e$ list of Fellows on y$^e$ other leaf, where he stands in 1632." ‡ Be this latter as it may, this Lectureship proved a complete success. "He did," says his Biographer, "with much diligence, and very great success, discharge that great work, to the spiritual edification and comfort of many yet alive, to whom his memory to this day is precious." § There are many other finely-informed words about this "ministry." They glow with a passionate affection. They are well worth being turned to. It is plain

* Letter from Rev. H. Cresswell, Canterbury, to myself.
† Clarke, as before, pp. 185, 186.   ‡ MSS. as before.
§ Clarke, as before, p. 185.

that " Master Herbert " was a *force* for good in the Community. He gave them not merely cups of " living water," but unsealed the very Fountain : and "in season and out of season," from his pulpit and in his " daily walk," by sermon and by catechising, by word and " letters," to the gentle and simple, in lane and manor, in the " huts where poor men lie," and in the " Mote" where his friend Viscount Maidstone lived, he emulated his Master "in doing good."— Very beautiful and intense after a noble type was this Canterbury residence. Fearless, fiery though softened, outspoken, having a firm grasp of his beliefs, resolute yet courteous, moved with deep yearnings for imperilled souls in vision of the awful " dark," and above all grandly confident of " the power unto salvation" of that Gospel which he preached ; his activity, his fervour, his *abandon* of utterance, his conflicts, his "enduring hardness," his pathos, his very wistful looks, seem to have left ineffaceable memories on his generation, and onward. Would that in these " latter days," one might recover his " weighty and powerful letters," (2 Cor. x. 10,) of which Clarke speaks as "yet to be seen in great numbers."\*

In 1632 he was presented by Laud to the vicarage of Ashwell in Hertfordshire. Let the Archbishop have all the benefit of this. † Here he continued the same " zeal, diligence, and care which he had before discovered, in seeking the good of those souls that were committed to him." His

\* Clarke, as before, p. 186. See *Baptist Register*, vol. i., pp. 258, 411, 503, for interesting extracts from Letters.

† Clarke having noted that Laud in his Defence named this as one of his "good deeds," Cole assails him with ludicrous acrimony. See MSS. as before. Cf also Laud. Works in Anglo-Catholic Library, vol. iv., p. 298, " History of the Troubles and Trial." Perhaps Laud has had scant justice done him in this and some other appointments : but it is preposterous in Cole to reflect upon Palmer, because of the reported sayings and observations of others.

biographer gives a singularly interesting account of (to quote the margin-headings) "his humility and sincerity," "his prudence," "his diligent catechising," "his prudent charity," "his manner of reforming disorders," "his family-government," "his care for sanctifying the Sabbath," "his secret duties," "his fasting and prayers," "his frequency in reading the Scriptures," and "his holy and exact walking."*

The following shews us an "interior" of the old Ashwell Vicarage that is winningly "lovely," (Philippians iv. 8,) and assures us that what Chaucer earlier and George Herbert later sang of "The Parson" was not an impossible ideal, but a bright and blessed reality :—We return upon Clarke.

"In the religious ordering of his own Family he was extraordinary vigilant and painful [=painstaking] that it might be so much as in him lay a garden without weeds; and that those which were under his roof might either not perish or at least not through his default. Indeed his house was a school of religion such as there are very few to be found; insomuch that it was counted a great happiness to live under his roof under the constant enjoyment of so much means for the soul's good.

"It was his great care to entertain none in his Family but such as were either truly godly, or at least willing to be instructed and educated in the ways of God, and who would be ready and willing to attend the exercises of God's worship, both publicly and privately, and to avoid all scandalous conversation.

"It was his constant practice twice every day to pray with his Family, not allowing any to be absent; at which times he read to them some portion both of the Old and New Testament.

"He was also careful to catechise his Family twice every

* Clarke, as before, pp. 188-191.

week, and likewise on Friday and Saturday to require an account from them of the Sermons preached the Lord's-day before, which he then repeated to them.

"Having also—while at Ashwell—the sons of divers considerable persons of the nobility and gentry sojourning in his house, for their better education in religion and learning, (he maintaining in his house an assistant as a schoolmaster to teach them,) he required of them the like account in catechising and repetitions as of his own servants.

"He had also daily after dinner and supper a chapter read by one of those gentlemen in course, and he whose turn was to read was required also, after he had read, to repeat the substance out of his memory, which, by constant custom, they had attained an ability to perform very exactly: after which himself used to go over the same briefly by way of exposition of what appeared difficult, and noting such observations as were most obvious from the most remarkable passages therein." *

Let any one of the sections of the above margin-headings in the old folio be dipped into and there will stand out as fine a specimen of the ancient Puritan gentleman as History shews, most meetly servant of Him, in the words of Dekker,

"A soft, meek, patient, humble, tranquil spirit,
The first true gentleman that ever breath'd."

Once more I must turn to Clarke to shew how truly he lived as under the "great Task-Master's eye."

"As he was very careful," he says, "to order all his actions according to his constant rule, of being subservient to the glory of God and the good of souls, so that even his journeys, visits, discourses and familiar converses with any, were not undertaken without a special eye hereunto; so did he also keep an exact account of what had passed, *every night before his going to rest*, setting down in writing, in his usual

* Clarke, as before, p. 190.

character, *the passages of that day, what actions or discourses he had been employed in,* what successes or disappointments, what mercies or crosses he met withal, and what failings he observed in himself: all which he surveyed again at the end of every week, writing down the chief passages of that week, and so from month to month and year to year. By means whereof he was thoroughly acquainted with his own spiritual condition and did maintain a constant exactness and even walking with God." \* In the italicised lines we have the prototype of Chatterton's Sir Charles Bawdin, who

> "Summ'd the actions of the day,
> Each night before he slept."†

In the same year—1632—with his presentation to Ashwell, having proceeded B.D. in 1630, he was, "by the University of Cambridge, made one of the University Preachers"—a "matter," observes Clarke, "of honour and repute rather than of profit or employment. Yet also a matter of some advantage in some cases, as times then went, being in the nature of a general licence, whereby he was authorized to preach as he should have occasion in any part of England."‡ He was also in association with Dr Tuckney, chosen a "Clerk" of the Convocation for the diocese of Lincoln.

BUT now we have reached the "time of change" and of "shaking"—1643. It were out of place to enter upon a narrative of the events that culminated in "The Commonwealth," with Oliver Cromwell, as its uncrowned king, grasping a truncheon mightier far than ever sceptre had or has been in "this England." Ours is a little literary service, not political, much less sectarian. We pass over therefore occurrences in which Herbert Palmer shared only in common with the mass of the Nation.

\* Clarke, as before, p. 191.  † Chatterton: "Bristow Tragedy," st. 42.
‡ Clarke, as before, p. 19.

But we must pause upon "The Assembly of Divines" at Westminster—a "council" that, let misinformed High Churchmen prate as they may, compares not ignobly with the greatest of them from the Nicene to the Tridentine; and to which, in its " Confession" and " Catechisms,"—compacting as they do those "things most surely believed among us,"—we in Scotland owe more in the shaping of our national religious character than to all other sources of influence—outside of the Word of God itself—put together.

Having been appointed by " The Parliament" a member of "The Assembly," he at once asserted for himself a foremost position among the foremost. He was chosen " one of the *Assessors*," whose office it was " to assist the Prolocutor in case of absence or infirmity." " He was in that Assembly," observes Clarke, "an eminent and very useful member, exceeding diligent and industrious, being very rarely absent, and that not but upon urgent, unavoidable occasions. For as he accounted it an honour to be employed by God in so public a service for the good of His Church: so he did conscientiously attend upon that service, preferring it before all other more particular employments, which, though in themselves excellent, yet ought, in his judgment, to give way to this."* Then follows "his fitness for it:" " He was exceeding well fitted for this employment, having a clear and ready apprehension, a firm and vast memory, a solid and steady judgment, and a good ability freely to express himself. In matters of deliberation he manifested much integrity and Christian wisdom. In matters of debate, whether about doctrine or discipline, he discovered a great sagacity in searching out the true sense of Scripture, a clear judgment and strength of reason, as well in the accurate stating of questions for debate as in confirming the truth and dissolving

* Clarke, as before, p. 192.

objections against it; in all, a great measure of zeal, piety, and prudence. All which procured him much reverence and esteem from the rest of his brethren, who judged his presence and assistance a very great help and advantage in that difficult work, and bewailed his death as an unspeakable loss."\*

In the "Journal" of "The Assembly" kept by the famous Dr John Lightfoot, and in the "Letters" during its sittings of Robert Baillie, Principal of the University of Glasgow, we obtain various interesting notices and glimpses of our Worthy. Some of these I would now present from the latter: with references to Lightfoot confirmatory and elucidative. Writing "Mr William Spang," under date December 7, 1643, he says, *inter alia:* "The Parliament became the other day sensible of their too long neglect of wryting to the Churches abroad of their condition; so it was the matter of our great committee to draw up letters in the name of the Assemblie for the Protestant Churches. *The drawing of them was committed to Mr Palmer, who yet* is upon them."† Thus those trumpet-tongued "Addresses" to the sister Churches, which are found in dim old quarto tractates, proceeded from the brave soul of our Palmer. They have the ring of Milton's State-Letters in them; and a Pauline fervour. Again: a little onward, to Dickson probably, information is given of the preparation of "A Directory of Worship," and "Mr Palmer" is the first name mentioned after the chairman,‡ and it emerges that "catechising" was specially committed to him.§ In the debate over "twentie long sessions" between the Independents, represented by Thomas Goodwin, Bridges, Burroughs, Nye, Simpson, and

---

\* Clarke, as before, p. 192.
† The Letters and Journals of Robert Baillie, A.M., &c. Edited from the Author's Manuscripts, by David Laing, Esq. Vol. ii., p. 111.
‡ Ibid., p. 117, 118.   § Ibid., p. 140.

Caryll, and the Presbyterians, on Church-government, "that many particular congregations were under the government of one Presbyterie," once more "Mr Palmer" was one of three chosen to "remeid" the "evills and satisfie the minds of all."\*—In a letter to "Mr Spang," the "Postscript" contains the well-known account of "a day of Fasting" with such "praying" and "preaching" as make your modern whimperers over a prayer longer than fifteen minutes, and sermon beyond half-an-hour, shudder. "Mr Palmer" was one of "the preachers."† Under date, August 18, 1644, we have this graphic description of his preaching along with one like-minded : "On Tuesday last there was a solemne Fast for Generall Essex's armie. Mr Palmer and Mr Hill did preach that day to the Assemblie, two of the most Scottish and free sermons that ever I heard anywhere. The way here of all preachers, even the best, has been, to speake before the Parliament with so profound a reverence as truelie took all edge from their exhortations, and made all applications to them toothless and adulatorious. That stile is much changed of late : however, *these two good men laid well about them, and charged publike and parliamentarie sins strictlie on the backs of the guilty;* among the rest their neglect to settle religion according to the Covenant, and to set up Ordination, which lay so long in their hands. *This was a means to make the House of Commons send us down that long-delayed paper of Ordination.*‡ Throughout, Baillie has evidently the profoundest regard for Palmer : and the whole movements of "The Assembly," as reflected in Lightfoot and elsewhere, shew that it was common to all.§

There were many remarkable men in "The Assembly"—

---

\* Baillie, as before, p. 145.  † Ibid., p. 184.  ‡ Ibid., pp. 220, 221
§ Cf. Lightfoot's "Journal," (Works by Pitman, vols. 8vo, 1824.) Vol. xiii., pp. 41, 87, 88, 92, 215, 239, 253, 277, 283, 291, 292, *et alibi.*

such a galaxy as had been in vain looked for elsewhere in that age—and some of them had no doubt more recondite learning, more mass of intellect, more splendour, more of sustained power to think out those gigantic problems that have perplexed an Augustine and an Athanasius, a Calvin, and a Leibnitz, more of the delicacies of a tender spiritualism; while there were others who striding up to "sinners," however highly seated, denounced them with a *momentum* to which our saintly and slight "Preacher" was unequal. Yet was it but the difference between light and lightning. His was the omnipotence of the light that touches and leaves still gleaming, the dew on the rose, and unruffled the delicate feather of a lark's wing—silent undisplaying might. That of more lauded names again may be likened to the fierce, terrible out-flash of the lightning which smites, and draws after it the bellowing thunders.

There were "certain points" in Church-government upon which in the outset Palmer was "unsatisfied," though on the whole he held to Presbyterianism. But "by the debates of the Assembly" he received "satisfaction."\* Cole has much ribaldry of abuse because of this: and shews thereby utter incapacity to understand a man of so much larger a mould of soul than his own narrow, royalistic, and ultra-Church one. The more's the pity that Southey and others have stooped to echo the same preposterous accusations of self-interested motives on the part of such Puritans as Palmer—men who were morbidly scrupulous lest they should swerve by a hair's-breadth from the line of conscience and truth.†

During the "sittings" of "The Assembly," an important communication was received from the Earl of Manchester. Principal Baillie thus speaks of it, April 2, 1644:—

\* Clarke, as before, p. 192.
† Southey, "Book of the Church," and Cole MSS., as before.

" When we were going to the rest of the propositions concerning the Presbyterie, my Lord Manchester wrote to us from Cambridge, what he had done in the University, how he had ejected for gross scandalls, the heads of five colledges, Dr Cosins, Beele, Sterne, Rainbow, and *ane other;* that he had made choice of five of our number, to be Masters in their places, *Mr Palmer,* Vines, Seaman, Arrowsmith, and our countreyman Young, requireing the Assemblie's approbation of his choise: which was unanimouslie given; for they are all very good and able divines."\* The "ane other," the learned editor of Baillie states was "Dr Lang:" but this seems a mistake, inasmuch as Palmer took the place of Dr Martin, who is not named. Of course, Royalists "cry out" of wrong because of this ejection: but "The Parliament" was the Government, and these displaced Masters were convicted traitors to *it.* .... Martin, Beale, and Sterne having been sent to the Tower as "active" in the dedication of the college-plate to the service of the king."† The College over which Palmer was thus made "Master" was his own, "Queen's:" and it is peculiarly satisfying to have "testimony" concerning his occupancy of the Mastership from one who will not be suspected of partiality to aught savouring of Puritanism, to wit, Symon Patrick, afterwards Bishop of Ely. In his "Account of his Life," we read :—

" I had not been long in the College before the Master,

\* Baillie, as before, p. 148.

† Fuller, Hist. of Camb., p. 169, 1655, folio. Cole's notice of Palmer's "Mastership" is very characteristic :—" Herbert Palmer, S.T.B., on ye ejection of Dr Martin, this man was put in by ye Earl of Manchester, and therefore is not reckoned among ye Masters of the College on ye aforesaid Table, where no notice is taken of him. However he was Master for 3 years, and therefore shall assign him a place in my Catalogue, tho' an Intruder." Heigho! Master Cole! But the Earl of Manchester had the "ordinance of the Parliament to make appointments:" and beshrew thy folly, knowing that, in writing 'Intruder' against a venerable name.

Mr Herbert Palmer, took some notice of me, and sent for me to transcribe some things for the press; and soon after made me the college scribe* which brought me a great deal of money, many leases being to be renewed. It was not long before I had one of the best scholarships in the college bestowed upon me; so that I was advanced to a higher rank, being made a pensioner. But before I was bachelor of arts, *this good man died, who was of an excellent spirit and was unwearied in doing good.* Though he was a little crooked man, yet he had such authority, that the fellows reverenced him as much as we did them, *going bare when he passed through the court*, which after *his* death was disused.

"I remember very well that being a member of the Assembly of Divines, he went off to London and sometimes stayed there a quarter of a year. But before he went, he was wont to cause the bell to be tolled, to summon us all to meet in the hall. There he made a pathetical speech to us, stirring us up to pious diligence in our studies, and told us, with such seriousness as made us believe, he should have as true an account from those he could trust, of the behaviour of every one of us in his absence as if he were here present with us to observe us himself. This, he said, we should certainly find true at his return. And truly he was as good as his word: for those youths whom he heard well of when he came back to college, he sent for to his lodgings and commended them; giving books to those that were well maintained, and money to the poorer sort. He was succeeded by a good man, (Dr Horton,) but not such a governor." † To find the truculent slanderer of the Puritans, the author of the so-called "*Friendly* Debate," thus lovingly and reverently recalling the Puritan and Presbyterian "Master" of Queen's argues no common power to attract, and a witchery of in-

* Simon Patrick, nominatus scriba per suffragium præsidentis, Feb. 17, 1645. Regr.: Coll.: Regin.
† Works by Taylor, vol. ix., pp. 415-417.

fluence that speaks volumes. Clarke expatiates with kindred warmth on his "government of the College," "his care to promote religion there," "his care to advance learning," "his charity," "his prudence," "his zeal," "his courage and faithfulness." These are margin-headings of some of the happiest and quaintest portions of the "Life."* His influence in the College, and indeed in the University, was commanding. He shewed increasingly a faculty of government, and thus stood the old Greek test, 'Ἀρχὴ ἄνδρα δείκνυται. His "walk" was that of Una, or of "the Lady" in "Comus."

His Herts "charge" went not uncared-for during his Assembly absences. "The ordinary exercise of the ministerial work there, together with the profits of the place, he put over to a godly and able divine."† But "unwilling to intermit the exercise of his ministerial function, he did at first preach occasionally—as he was requested—in divers Churches in and about London, resolving notwithstanding within himself to accept of the first invitation for the constant exercise thereof. And, accordingly, being soon after requested by the inhabitants of Duke's place in London—who were then destitute of a minister—to preach amongst them, he did—notwithstanding their inability to raise any considerable maintenance which might invite him—willingly accept of that employment." ‡

His "ministry" here as everywhere else was an immediate and sustained success. We must allow Clarke to tell it: "This work he performed amongst them with much faithfulness and diligence, as well by public reading, praying and preaching amongst them twice every Lord's-day, and at other times as there was occasion ; as also by administering the Sacraments, public Catechising, and exposition of such portions of Scripture as were read amongst them. And likewise, as his custom had been elsewhere, by more

\* Clarke, as before, pp. 196-199.   † Ibid., p. 193.   ‡ Ibid.

private acquaintance and converse with them in their families, whereby he might be the better able to afford personal directions and other ministerial helps to them as their several conditions might require. All which was performed with so much meekness, wisdom, and piety, and accompanied with such a blessing from God, as that it made a very great impression on them for their good, and was entertained by them with much approbation and affection, they being ambitious who should enjoy most of his heavenly communion and converse with him."*

But a star so brilliant could not be permitted to shine on so low and level a horizon. When the "new Church"—gray and venerable now—at Westminster "was perfected and made fit for use, the inhabitants there, and others concerned therein, did sollicite him to undergo the charge of that great people." Then followed a sensitive "case of conscience," such as it does one good to read in this far-off day: while one is indignant on finding a Cole fouling it with his pitiable libels, as a snail a passion-flower.† The final result was, that the Scottish tutor of John Milton, Dr Thomas Young, having been transferred to "Duke's place," Palmer accepted Westminster. Here he continued the same "burning and shining" course, "insomuch," observes his Biographer, "that it seems almost a miracle that so weak a body as his should possibly be able to do so much as constantly he performed, continuing ofttimes to speak in public *for the space of six or eight hours* on a Sabbath-day, besides much time spent in more private exercises of prayer, repetitions, &c., in the family. Yet when his friends have persuaded him to favour himself, judging so much pains to be more than his body could endure, his answer hath been, that his strength would spend of

* Clarke, as before, p. 193.
† Cole mocks and scoffs at the idea of any "scruples" here, as in the case of his "points" in The Assembly. Faugh!

itself though he did nothing, and it could not be better spent than in God's service."* His zeal in "conversing" with "the nobility and gentry" in their own homes received a rich reward. "Very many of them are ready upon all occasions to profess that it was their happiness to be acquainted with him, and bewail the want of it as a great loss."† His skill and kindliness in dealing with the "ignorant," and those "out of the way," were remarkable. His prudence, his charity, his thoughtfulness, his suavity, his unvarying gentlemanliness, his living-out himself of what he taught, his ubiquity of oversight, his pleasantness, his holiness, his meekness, his loveableness, came out in every sphere he occupied. Speaking of the several treatises which compose our reprint, and giving as its margin-heading "a true Nathanael," Clarke remarks: "That his constant practice was so exactly consonant to the strict principles that are there expressed, as can hardly be believed by those that have not seen it." And then: "He was a man indeed of a very public spirit, and wholly laid himself out for God: and therefore, though he was ready to deny himself, and condescend freely when his own interest was only concerned, yet was he zealous and tenacious in things that concerned God's glory, reserving his heat to encounter sin."‡ With reference to his titled and illustrious audience at St Margaret's, Westminster, he was wont to say, "he did not in that place preach BEFORE them, (*ut coram judice,*) but TO them, (*authoritative,*) as by commission from God."§ Altogether, a more Pauline man—physically and spiritually—we can scarcely conceive. Even from our faint blurred lines it must appear that in HERBERT PALMER we have a very remarkable man, of whose thoughts and speculations, written and spoken words, and beautiful life, it were well if the 19th century knew more.

\* As before, p. 194.   † Ibid., pp. 194, 195.
‡ Ibid., p. 19.   § Ibid., p. 199.

"The time of his sickness was not long." He died with "blessings" and "prayers" for all, and with pathetic humility, in 1647, in the 46th year of his age. He was interred in the "New Church at Westminster." *

It needeth not that we offer any general summary or estimate of the "character" of Herbert Palmer. That must have come out to the most cursory reader in the progress of our little Memoir. But it may be observed, in a sentence, that while his published writings are limited to a few occasional "Sermons" and tractates—his largest being the first part of the "Sabbatum Redivivum," in association with Cawdrey—there is nevertheless sufficient to shew that his contemporary renown and reverence rested on no fortuitous base. There is depth as well as breadth, and an intense grasp of whatever he handles. Occasionally gleams of beauty illumine a massive argument—snatches of melody a seer-like exposure of sin. You have the conviction of reserved power throughout; and behind many a noble unfolding of "the way, the truth, and the life," you get a sight of the preacher on his knees. You have the feeling also that not a few of the conclusions reached have been the issue of profound meditation, not unvisited by speculation, not untempted of doubt. You see that he is one who looked into the "heart of things." But the main characteristic that impresses itself is the unearthly "holiness" of the man—the grand reality of his "Life" with God—and when Laud—not unnaturally perhaps—declined his attendance in the Tower and at the block he "unawares" refused to "entertain an angel."† Of his personal appear-

---

* Curiously enough, the exact date—day and month of his death,—is not given. But his successor at Ashwell, Mr John Crowe, was appointed on 28th Sept. 1647.—*Journal of House of Commons*, v. 320.

† Cf. Laud, Works, Anglo-Catholic Library, *sub nomine*, specially iv. 424.

ance the photographic portrait prefixed to the 100 large-paper copies of our reprint will convey an idea. Referring to it, Cole says, "I forgot to mention that there is a tolerable good print of him in Clarke's book, which shews him to be a puny kind of man and crooked."* The old sarcasm, παρουσία τοῦ σώματος ἀσθενής, (2 Cor. x. 10.) Still he must have been of no great bodily presence: and perchance was of Aristotle's mind for Aristotle's reason, Ἄνοος ὁ μακρός.† We have an anecdote confirmatory of his "little stature" and outwardly unimpressive look, and of the transfiguration which his speaking effected. I give it in the words of Clarke: "It is memorable that an ancient French gentlewoman, when she saw him the first time coming into the pulpit, being startled at the smallness of his personal appearance and the weakness of his look, cried out, in the hearing of those that sate by her, "Hola! *que nous dira cest enfant icy?*—Alas! what should this child say to us? But having heard him pray and preach with so much spiritual strength and vigour she lifts her hands to heaven with admiration and joy, blessing God for what she had heard."‡ Even the old "print" shews a body "o'er informed" by the burning soul within. There is a worn, wistful, sad forth-look that is unspeakably touching.

The many-wreathed head of Bacon can well spare the few green leaves of the authorship of "The Paradoxes;" and so we gladly place them around that of HERBERT PALMER.

ALEXANDER B. GROSART.

NOTE.—While this is passing through the press, an obliging communication reaches me from Charles H. Cooper, Esq., of Cambridge.

---

\* MSS. as before, in British Museum.
† In Physiogn. he approves the proverb.
‡ As before, p. 187.

The following are the exact dates of Palmer's progress at the University:—

St John's: Matriculated as a f. commoner, 23d March, 1615-16.
        B.A., 1618-19.
        M.A., 1622.
Queen's: Admitted f. commoner, 16th Dec. 1622.
        Admitted *tanquam socius*, 17th July, 1623, under royal mandate.
        B.D., 1631.
        President, 1644.
        Gave 30 vols. to Qu. Col. Library ("Restituta" iv. 366.)

Mr Cooper adds, "It is said that he was buried in New Chapel at Westminster, but his death is recorded in the register of S. Mary the Less, Cambridge, [Queen's Col. is not in that parish.] In the register is also recorded the burial, on 2d Jan. 1629-30, of Alice, wife to Dr Palmer. This Mrs Alice Palmer gave the parish a silver flagon and chalice." Whatever may be the explanation of the above entry, it is certain that he died in London, and was buried in New Church, Westminster. Clarke, who wrote from personal knowledge, could not possibly be mistaken. Moreover, Phil. Taverner, of Exeter College, Oxford, who is said to have written the "Brief Account" prefixed to the 10th edition of the "Memorials," confirms his account. As Palmer was unmarried, this "Alice" must have been "wife" of some other Palmer. The Cambridge register *above* supplies the exact date of his death—viz., August 13.     G.

## NOTE.

The following is the title-page of the first edition of the "Memorials," which consisted of Part I. only:—

Memorials
of
Godlinesse
and
Christianitie,
Part I.,
*Of making Religion one's Businesse.*

A Meditation, first communicated in a Letter to a private Friend, and now offered to all as a Patterne of what all should make their desire and endeavour.

By Herbert Palmer, B.D.,

London.
Printed by G. M. for *Tho. Underhill*, at the Bible in Woodstreet, 1644.

Title. To the Reader, pp. 3, [unpaged] and pp. 55. In the British Museum copy there is written on title-page, by a contemporary hand "Jan. 3" as the date of publication.

To the 13th edition of the whole (1708) the excellent William Tong prefixed this characteristic preface:—

" We live in an age wherein little names must sometimes be made use of to revive the memory of great ones; the ingratitude of the world so soon forgetting its best friends and her efactors, makes this custom necessary, otherwise I should never have assumed to myself the honour of recommending these excellent Memorials of the Reverend Mr Herbert Palmer, a person in every way eminent not only for his great parentage and learning, but especially for his holy zeal and unwearied diligence in the service of God and of the souls of men, that we may safely venture to say, few ages of the Church have produced his equal, scarce any his superior.

" His most instructive Life has been long since published among many others of Christ's Worthies; but that noble and Divine Spirit that made him so much to excel, will be best discerned by a serious perusal of these his Remains, which, like himself, are much, very much in a little. That they may be blessed of God to the restoring of a truly evangelical temper and life in us all, is the desire of an unworthy servant of our blessed Redeemer.—W. TONG." G.

# MEMORIALS
OF
Godlines & Christianity.

In three Parts.

PART I.

*CONTAINING*

MEDITATIONS

1. *Of making Religion ones Business.*
2. *An Appendix applied to the Calling of a Minister.*

The fifth Edition corrected and enlarged by the AUTHOR

HERBERT PALMER, B.D. late Master of *Qu. Coll.* Camb.

*LONDON,*

Printed by *A.M.* for *T.Underhill* at the Anchor in *Pauls* Church-yard, 1655.

I Conceive this Letter, with the *Appendix* following it, to be very well worthy the Printing.*

---

\* The name of the Licenser, "Charles Herle," is, singularly enough, dropped out in the Fifth Edition; it duly appears in others. G.

## TO THE READER.

CHRISTIAN READER,

THIS ensuing Meditation upon " making Religion ones busines," having first affected my own heart, and afterward some friends to whom it hath been communicated; I have been so far made to believe, that by God's blessing it may be some advancement to the busines of Religion, now in this season, when Religion hath Retainers enough, but not Servants enough; that at last my thoughts told me, The very expressions herein would upbraid me as not true to them, if I had denied, or longer delayed their publication. I have no doubt but sundry passages in them, will meet with some scoffs and some cavils, as being overnice and precise; and I shall meet with some reproaches, as not answering my own strict rules. But in hopes there will yet be found those, that will both be glad to see such a piece of a patern for their Hearts and Lives, and also strive to make it their own in affection and practice; I have resolved to adventure the one and the other: and do trust also that by God's grace, it will somewhat help to make me the more watchfull over my own self and my behaviour, that I may not only not shame my self and my so publick professions, but also may set a Real Copy in some proportion sutable to this Verbal one, for thy double benefit. Herein if thou wilt help me still with thy prayers (as I am confident thou wilt, if thou reap any benefit by it) I again tell thee, thou maist be the better for it thy self, while I am thereby through God's mercy to us both, helped to do thee yet some further spiritual Service, which while I live, I must now alway profess my self ambitious of, as being ever,

Thine and the Churches servant

in Christ altogether,

Dec. 13, 1644.                                     HERBERT PALMER.

## OF MAKING RELIGION ONES BUSINESS.

MY true Friend, It hath been an usual saying with me, (would God I could ever have the feeling of it in my self,) *That the character of a godly man, is to make Religion his business.*
I will now a little descant upon it, so as to set down what I should and would do in this kinde. I shall set a copy, at least to teach my self, and provide a remembrancer to quicken my frequent dulnesses.

1. I desire to have *my affections all molded by religion;* and towards it, my thoughts and words and deeds, to be all exercises of religion, and my very cessation from works commanded by religion, and limited and circumstantiated by religion: my eating, drinking, sleeping, journeying, visiting, entertaining of friends, to be all directed by religion: And that above all, I may be serious and busie in the acts of religion, about the Word, prayer, praises, singing, sacraments; not only that the duties in each kinde be performed, but religiously performed, with life and vigour, with faith, humility and charity.

2. To these ends, I desire my heart may be possessed with these two fundamental principles.

(1.) *That religion is the end of my creation*, and of all the benefits, not onely spiritual, but temporal, which God bestows upon me.

(2.) *That religion is my felicity*, even for the present;

though derived from that eternal felicity, which is now laid up for me, and to be hereafter possessed by me in heaven: so glorious is that felicity, that from the first moment of our interest in it, it casts a lightsome gladsome brightnesse upon the soul, even many years sometimes before the enjoyment of the fulnesse of it: like to the sunne shedding forth his fore-running beams to enlighten all our part of the world, many minutes before his full light offers it self to our eye.

3. When I speak thus *of religion to be felicity*, I mean it of God and Christ, the object of religion: without whom, religion is but an empty name, a pernicious errour. But as religion is, "to know God, and Him whom he hath sent, Jesus Christ,"* it is eternal life begun now here below; but never to end in any time or place.

4. I wish *these thoughts may meet me first in the morning*, as worldly-minded mens businesses do them: that I may count all things but interruptions till my minde be setled in its course for that day, and that my minde be so setled and habituated in those purposes, that it may be readily in order ordinarily, and only need time for solemn performance of religious duties, and for extraordinary projects.

5. Specially, I wish, as I am bound by millions of eternal obligations, *That I may love the Lord my God, Christ Jesus my Redeemer,* " with all my heart, with all my soul, with all my minde, with all my strength,"† to the utmost extent of all these phrases: and that to make my minde more apprehensive of them, I may not prophane any of them, by using to say in slight matters, " I love such a thing with all my heart," or " I will do such a thing with all my heart." It may seem a nicety to check such a phrase: but I read this morning, (Prov. vii. 2,) " Keep my commandments, and live, and my law as the apple of thine eye." Which sentence by God's blessing hath occasioned this whole Meditation, whatever it is. The

* John xvii. 3. G.        † Matt. xxii. 37. G.

"apple of the eye" is the tenderest thing in the world of natural things; the law of God no lesse, infinitely more, in spirituals. As I therefore like not the word "infinite" but when we speak of God: so those forenamed phrases seem to be God's peculiar: and that one main cause, why common men so readily say, "They love God with all their heart," (I mean, why they so easily deceive themselves in so saying) is, because they have adulterated the phrase "with all my heart," and prostituted it to every base trifle. Say, if it be not so. And then as Saint James blames for not saying, "If the Lord will," &c., though every one will grant such words necessary, and pretend to suppose them: so is it not blame-worthy to say in petty matters, what should make a sacred sound in our ears, and to our spirits?*

6. I wish *I could lose my self in a holy trance of meditation, every time I think of God and Christ*, as the Authour, Fountain, Life, Substance of all my happiness; all-sufficient, alone-sufficient, onely-sufficient for my soul, and all comfort and good. Nothing wanting in God and Christ to eternity! No need of any creature: no accession by any creature: no one creature, not all of them comparable to him, or anything without him. Time lost, happiness lost, while converse with any creature, further than according to his ordinance, as his instruments and servants.

7. I wish *I could forget all respects to my self, carnal, natural, while I have any service to perform to God*, as I have every moment, though I cannot ever think so, that I might shew I love God with strength, "my God with all my strength," and never be weary; of his immediate services specially: or if naturally, yet not spiritually. Lusts are vigorous, when the body languishes, being spent. Oh, why is not grace more strong!

8. I wish *my heart may never recoil upon me*, with saying,

* See Note *a*. at end. G.

"Thou mightest now or such a time, have done thy God, thy Saviour more service than thou didst; even when thou didst somewhat, thy body and spirits would have held out longer time, and endured a greater stress of zeal." And much less, "Thou didst wholly lose such an opportunity of doing or receiving good," (though scarce can any one do good, who receives not some present paiment, at least in soul, the enlargement of grace and holy affections;) and least of all, "Thou didst wholly employ thy strength to sinne;" or, "Thou hast weakned thy strength by intemperance, or any other foolish or sinfull practice."

9. I wish that every day among my first thoughts, one may be, *What special businesse have I within doors ?* Within my soul, what sin to mortifie? whether lately raging, and even but last day or night prevailing over me? or which I have had (at least some late) victories over? that I may allot time to pursue it, and by no means forget it in my prayer, and arm myself against the encounter, if there be any possibility of my being assaulted that day. And what grace to strengthen? wherein I have been exceeding feeble of late? or even begun to obtain some vigour? which it may easily be lost, and will be, if not with all care and means, and prayers, fomented and cherished ; that so I may prepare for it : these are a Christian's main businesses within himself alwaies.

10. Withall, I wish "*to die daily.*"\* I mean not, that I daily wish for death ; but that I may foresee it more than possible, and may prepare for it, resolvedly, contentedly : that I may look at it, as at a means of happiness, and take such order as it may not cut me off from any main necessary imployment : but each hour and minute to dispatch the substantials of my business, and referre circumstances and events to the All-wise, powerfull, and gracious Providence of the

\* 1 Cor. xv. 31. G.

great Ruler, and King of the whole world, and of every creature.

11. I wish *to improve every relation I stand in towards any of mankinde, to the advancement of religion:* that glory may redound to Christ, by my being a childe to one, a brother to another, a neighbour to a third, a kinsman, a friend, an acquaintance to any one: that as well for the credit of religion (which commands to give to all their due honour,* and to love them as myself) as for the propagation of religion, I may be ambitious to approve myself the best childe, or subject, or friend, &c., in the world: and careful also, to insinuate myself, as much as may be, into the favour of every one I converse withall in the world, of superiours, by submission and diligence: of equals, by courtesie and freedom: of inferiours, by affability mixt with gravity, and gentleness, with necessary strictness. And that I may not fail to entitle God to what ever ground I gain upon the affections of any; that is, to engage them thereby the more forwardly in His service, in their own persons, and towards all others, and that I myself also may reap some spiritual benefit by them, that so I may bless God for them, and they Him for me, and others for them and me together.

12. Particularly, I wish, *that toward inferiours, I may never put lesse, but rather more weight upon God's commandments than mine own, and upon religious than civil observances:* and that because the best are not angels I may bear with more patience, failings in meer worldly, than spiritual matters.

13. I wish *never to be one of those that feed themselves without fear;* but that "whether I eat or drink, I may do all to the glory of my God;"† that is, seasonably, sparingly, and with choice; for health and strength: not gluttony, drunkennesse, or riotous curiosity. That I may daily remember my

\* Rom. xiii. 7. G.     † 1 Cor. x. 31. G.

businesse, not to be to live to eat, but eat to live; that I may follow my busines, that is, Christianity: that I may not forget, how slippery a place the throat is, and how easily that glides down, which after works disease: that because the craving of the sensual appetite, seeming but reasonable, being but for one's self, is oft the betraying of reason itself, besides the quelling of grace. Both grace and reason may combine together in the practice of this difficultest piece of self-denial. And that I may ever consider, not only what a shame, what an unthankfulnesse it is in the least degree to disable myself for the service of Him, who allows me liberally so much as can be fit for me, how much soever that be; but also what pity to waste good creatures to so vile a purpose, as to weaken my body, or overcharge my spirits, with what was meant to strengthen and quicken them. That from the observation of the untowardness of my minde, when it is in the best temper, I may tremble at the thoughts of the least intemperance, which if it fetter not my body, so as it cannot do its duty, will at least hamper my wits, and many times take away from me the will to go about it aright. That therefore I may count all inordination or immoderation in meat or drink, poison at least to my soul, and in a degree also to my body, as is confest by all, some meats and drinks to be in themselves to some, and others, if taken to such a quantity.

14. I wish *to be watchful over my self alwaies, that I may be thus sober;* \* and sober, that I may be watchful; and watchful, that I may withstand enemies, and have time and spirits to do all the works my heavenly Master sets me about.

15. I wish *to redeem all time I can from sleep;* and so to order my sleep, as I may redeem most time. To redeem all time I can from sports; and so to order my imploy-

\* 1 Pet. v. 8.  G.

ments, as that the varieties of them may commonly be recreation, enough, without using any sports at all, for my mindes sake : and that if my body seem necessarily to require any, I may remember that Nature is content with a little, and Grace never asks more. That if courtesie require me to bear friends company in their sports, I may not only refuse such as are unlawfull in themselves, but in others, consider whether they are not for the present unseasonable, or vitiated with some other ill circumstances ; being specially shie of those that are apt to leade astray, either by affording provocations to impatience, or threatning to swallow up too much time, of which friends not seldom robbing us, do it no way more than by exacting of us to hold out with them in their sports ; which they by an evil, though significant name, usually call " Pastimes."*

16. I wish *to redeem all time from vain thoughts and unprofitable musings:* upon my bed night or morning, in my walking or riding upon the way, in my attendances where neither my eye nor my tongue can be profitably set on work ; and to take those advantages greedily to advance the businesses of God and my soul. My thoughts are her eldest and noblest offspring ; and so too worthy to be cast away upon base objects.

17. I wish *to redeem all time from idle words and frivolous discourses;* to avoid what I can the hearing of such pratlings; to shun all light and frothy, and amatorious† books. My tongue is " my glory,"‡ and my best instrument to advance the glory of God and religion towards others. It were pity to prophane it with such words, as to be upon my contrary score at the day of accounts : and so much I have to learn of God and of religion, as without slighting them, I can finde no leisure to give heed to trifles, besides the danger

\* See Note *b.* at end. G.     † See Note *c.* at end. G.
‡ Ps. xvi. 9. G.

of poison to be conveyed in these. If I were confined to the society of Pagans, I might from thence expect some profitable discourse, though altogether of the world; and even towards them I were bound to offer, at least sometimes, mention of God. How much more among such as call themselves Christians! Specially, who professe Christianity to be their businesse as well as mine.

18. I desire *to redeem all time I can from curiosity in dressing my body*, as that which besides the vanity and unprofitableness, endangers the leaving off (the best cloathing) humility, and so doubly sets my business back.

19. I wish *to redeem what time I can, even from worldly businesses*, whatever they are; so as at least I may never want room to "exercise myself unto godliness;"* to perform my daily solemn services to God, both personal and domestick, and for extraordinary projects to the honour of God.

20. I desire *to take no journey, or make no visit, which fals not into the road of religion.* Courtesie, which to allow, and in a sort, even command, is religious honour, will carry me a little way, sometimes: but specially, purposes, accompanied with hopes, of making all my correspondencies pay tribute to religion, whilest in the mean time, I am carefull to lose no opportunity of trafficking for religion's gain, and resolutely to stay no longer time any where, than while I may do my self or others, more good there, than in another place.

21. I wish specially *to make all my medlings in worldly businesses serviceable to religion:* whilest I imploy whatever talent I have received, and do receive, to strengthen, encourage, and secure myself, family, friends, neighbours, and all fellow-Christians, in the waies of godliness; and to exercise and demonstrate faith, humility, patience, contentednes, liberality, justice, heavenly-mindedness in the midst of worldy imploiments, and thereby to draw even strangers to admire and

* 1 Tim. iv. 7.  G.

approve of that religion, which teaches and effectually persuades so much good.

22. Particularly, I wish that *I may never grasp so much of the world as to distract my head with cares, or engage my heart in sins*, and that in the rust that cleaves to my fingers in telling of money though each peece seem clean enough, I may see the emblem of the defilement, gotten insensibly by the use even of lawful things, that therefore I may constantly afterwards wash my heart by prayers and meditations.

23. I wish *to account nothing a crosse to me, but what crosses religion* in some respect, either to my own soul or others; to reckon by that rule, my losses and gains, my thrivings and goings back: and for this reason, to esteem scandall\* the worst of evils; and to give, or do, or suffer any thing to prevent or take them away: and next to these the want of God's ordinances.

24. I wish *to have my heart and conversation alwaies in heaven*, as counting "my treasure to be laid up there;" † and though I must trade with worldly commodities, yet to reckon grace my chief stock: and that as fore-seeing losses, I may trade much in the assurance-office, and study daily the art of Christian alchymy, which can extract advantage out of losses, gold out of every thing, even dung itself; that is, grace not only out of every gracious act of God's providence within sight or hearing; but even out of afflictions and very sins.

25. Particularly, I wish *to improve the time of sicknesse*, which disables from most worldly businesses, to set forward greatly the businesses of God and my soul: and wholly to bestow that leisure upon them, further than the necessity of my body cals me, partly to attend it: and that because I am then debar'd from publick means of thriving, I may

\* That is, putting a "stumbling stock" in the way of others. G.
† Matt. vi. 21. G.

beg of every visitant, to help me with somewhat; which yet will not impoverish, but help to enrich them also, by mutuall trading in spirituall matters:* and to count this covetousness only lawful, never to think I have enough of grace, but the lesse time I have to live, the more greedy to be to heap up of these riches.

26. I desire *to count the Sabbath, the Lord's day, mine;* made for me, for mine advantage, the market-day for my soul, a spiritual harvest day, wherein I may all day long make provision, and lay up in store for afterwards, and to bless God continually for it, as without which my soul might be in danger to starve, either through want of publick provisions, or leisure to provide for my self what might be had: and therefore by no means to overslip the opportunity, even for my own sake, besides the commandment: and to take to the utmost minute that I can, my spiritual liberty to serve God, and get grace, not allowing any thing by my good will to interrupt me therein.

27. I desire *to account the sacrament of the Lord's Supper a singular fair,* wherein the "bread that came down from heaven,"† the water of life, spiritual wine and milk, and whatsoever else is nourishing and comfortable to the soul, is freely offered, and to be had "without money, and without price."‡ That therefore I may be sure not to miss, when I may go to it. And yet, because all that come thither make not so happy a bargain, but rather purchase to themselves wrath and judgement, I may be carefull to prepare my self so by examination, that my soul be not sent away fasting, or which is worse, poisoned, while my body is entertained.

28. I desire *to account all other ordinances of God* (in their degree and manner likewise) *the means of my soul's enriching, nourishing physick:* so that if I should slight or trifle away

* See note *d.* at end. G.     † John vi. 32, 33. G.
‡ Isa. lv. 1. G.

these blessed opportunities, I could not but die a beggar, die and starve, die a miserable diseased leper, die and perish eternally. That therefore I may not be so much a fool, as to have these put as prizes into my hand to get wisdom withall, and I to have no heart to them : or that pretending no other errand to the place where they are, nor other business at that time, but to receive them, I should be so wickedly mad as to sleep away the offers of grace then tendered unto me, or suffer my minde to be diverted to any other thing, or to look that God should hear me where I scarce hear my self in my prayers, or refuse to hear Him in His word.

29. I desire *to account those my best friends that most help me in my business of Christianity;* and to esteem a watchful consideration and faithful admonitions, the most necessary and best expressions of friendship, and best helps to my feeble and frail minde.

30. I desire *if ever I marry, to account that one of the greatest businesses even of religion,* that I can undertake any time in my whole life ; which if I speed well in, will incomparably (beyond that other men or creatures can) advance my spiritual projects and advantages ; and contrarily disappoint and overthrow them, if I make an ill match : that therefore being truly sensible of my own naturall sinfull inclination, which may betray me as soon as any other, into some one, at least, of those many untoward courses, which persons of all qualities and conditions usually take on this occasion ; as also apprehensive of God's punishing no sin more frequently or sharply in this world, I may from the first moment of my entertaining any such thoughts make my most ardent and faithfull prayers keep pace with them ; first to implore to be directed in a perfect way, and then to be blessed with a true helper every way meet for me.

31. Particularly, I desire that the phrases of " marrying

in the Lord," and "not being unequally yoaked,"\* &c. (not corrupted by the world's false glosses, but truly interpreted by a serious conscience) may ever have an absolute negative voice in all propositions, that is, that I may never marry with any whom I have reason to judge not to be truly religious; whilest yet I conclude, that religion alone is not sufficient to make any match. That I may never dare to crosse the rules of nature in too much disparity of age, or in robbing parents of their right, at least of approbation and consent; nor those of civility, by aspiring too eminently above my degree, or debasing my self too much below it; withall counting it a necessary qualification in one whom I may match myself unto, to have no predominant humour which I cannot bear, but to be able to bear any infirmity of mine, and to be, at least, some help to my spirit in those things wherein I specially need help.

32. I desire (for my security in all these resolutions,) *that I may never be in haste*, but make a leasurable† and sufficient enquiry by myself and friends, answerable to the necessity which the world's deceitfulnesse enforces in a business of such lasting importance; but specially, that I may never be in love (with the estate or comelinesse of person) which would hinder any full enquiry, and stop my ears to any (though never so true an) information; and blinde my eyes from a right discerning, whether there be indeed that which in others I was wont to make the character of piety: and even in a visible observation of defects, make me wickedly run to God's decree for my excuse, and say, marriages are made in heaven, or presumptuously promise my self that I shall make them better, when once married, and headlong run on, notwithstanding all the contrary advice of friends, or even the commands of parents, and be in

---

\* 1 Cor. vii. 39, and 2 Cor. vi. 14. G.
† See Note *e*. at end. G.

danger to have my heart broke with discontent, if the Providence of God shall any way break the match; which last consideration forbids also too much engagement of affection upon the most worthy and fit person in the world, while there remains any possibility of dissolving the treaty.

33. I desire *to enforce the undervaluing of wealth or beauty* upon my spirit, from the scarcity of those who have all the other more necessary qualifications: and that remembring among all the ends of marriage mentioned in Scripture, none of them to be to make one rich, I may never consent to sell my liberty, my comfort, my self, for so long a term as during life, to make never so great a purchase of worldly estate: as also, though I must never match my self to any, till I can love their person, I may yet count it a sin to refuse one otherwise every way fit for me, upon the meer exception, that I cannot love, when there is no remarkable deformity to breed a loathing; and to reckon it a duty to pray earnestly to God to rectifie such untowardnesse of my minde, as makes me, without just cause, reject a gracious offer of his Providence towards me: and that to prevent the mischief of an unexpected continuall jarre all our lives long, I may be willing to be enquired into my self, as well as to enquire after others; and may not dissemblingly disguise, for a fit, that which will afterwards come certainly to be known; expecting that that love cannot be firm, whose foundation is laid upon a lie; but that I may, by my self or friends, fully and freely, before engagement be past, expresse what I expect, both for piety, and all other matters, of habitation, manner of living, order of family, and the like: and what may be expected from me in each respect; not fearing that this faithfulnesse to my self and them, should make a breach; but resolving that if this would break the match, being unconcluded, there would be no lesse danger that it would break the peace afterward, when

the unfaithfulnesse should be discovered: and that that breaking of the match were so much to be preferred before this breach of peace, by how much a cross is to be preferred before a sinne; and I cannot be a Christian, if I believe not that God can provide better for me, and will, if I yield up my will and all my affections wholly to him.

34. I desire *to let no day passe without once, at least, solemn casting up my accounts,* how my soul hath sped that day, and my business gone forward or backward; and to allot speciall times for a more full reckoning of many dayes, and summing up my whole stock of grace: so shall I be sure never to become a bankrupt, but compound for my debts in time, before I be sued, pursued to extremity.

Lastly, I desire *to account my Suretie's satisfaction my best riches,* and to treasure up charily* in my heart, my acquittances sealed with his bloud: and to fetch from his store all needful grace from time to time: His alsufficiency alone on all occasions must furnish me with "wisdom, righteousnesse, sanctification, redemption;"† he is and must be "all in all" to me, to Him, with the Father, and the Holy Ghost, be all glory, and love, and faith, and obedience rendred for ever. Amen.

    * See Note *f.* at end. G.    † 1 Cor. i. 30. G.

# AN APPENDIX APPLIED TO THE CALLING OF A MINISTER.

1. DESIRE specially *to improve my calling of a minister to the advancement of religion, both in my own and others' hearts.* Whatever calling I had, I were bound so to direct it: but this was erected to that purpose immediately, and no other, to found men in religion, and build them up in it. As therefore I must first account, that of me is required a greater forwardnesse in religion, and higher degree of heavenly-mindednesse, and being to the glory of Christ, than of ordinary Christians; because while their calling oft distracts and disturbs them from thinking of God and Christ, mine leades me directly to it; and those notions which they through ignorance or disuse are strangers to, I am happily necessitated to make familiar to me: so though I may yet have imperfections, I pretend religion in vain, if I allow my self in carelessenesse or unprofitablenesse in that profession of mine, the very exercise whereof is among the mainest businesses of religion, and which therefore in the preparations for it, and exercise of it, challenges all my strength of affections and spirits. If God should have given me my choice of all the employments the world knows, I could not wish any other, to do at once most good to my soul; and express what good I get, to do others' souls good also, and most shew my love to Christ and

Christians, in thankfulness for all that good I have and look for, both to my soul and body.

2. I desire therefore *to esteem it among the highest favours, among the greatest honours, so to be set on work*, specially with successe: and to make it appear that I do so esteem it, by putting forth all my abilities, that there may be no want in me, if successe follow not towards others. All the time my Saviour lived his first life upon earth, after his baptism (till he was to prepare himself for the sacrifice of his death) he undertook no other calling than this, and after his resurrection again practised it, so long as he conversed with men here below.* O let my heart therefore be so possest with his Spirit, that though my body must needs have its naturall supplies in due season, yet I may ever, as he did, count it "my meat and drink" to fulfill and finish this work;† and my recreation to go about doing good. And therefore though his Sabbath, the Lord's day, be according to nature the day of my greatest toil; yet because that day I most advance the businesse of his kingdom, and my own soul together, I may with more affections than others can, call the Sabbath "a delight," and triumph in it, not onely as a day of liberty, but of conquest and victory.

3. I desire *to extend the labours of my function beyond the expectation of those to whom they are to be directed.* I mean, not ever (yet sometimes) specially for length, but frequency, to be instant in season, and out of season, *volentibus, nolentibus*. And to rejoyce therefore, and only therefore, in the multitude of hearers, because among many there is more hope of doing some good, whilest yet I never suffer my self to be discouraged by their paucity, since God's grace is not tied to expect the help of a croud; and one soul gained or confirmed is worth an age of pains.

\* See note *g*. at end. G.     † John iv. 34. G.

4. I desire *in all the publick exercises of my ministry to suit my matter, method, phrase, repetition, and all other circumstances, so as I may be best understood and remembred, and may best convince and perswade every man's conscience,* and not to own one tittle or syllable that might hinder this in any: remembring herein my business to be not to broake\* for my own credit: but to deliver the messages of him who is no respecter of persons, but esteems the meanest soul worth shedding his bloud for, as well as the greatest.

5. I desire therefore *no more to neglect the instruction of the poorest childe, or the visiting of the most contemptible creature within my charge, than of the richest and noblest;* rather those of the eminenter sort may better spare me; because they may for themselves and theirs have more means and comforts than others can.

6. Specially, I desire *not to omit the advantage of any one's being sick:* because, (1.) Then they may have more leisure to ponder on any good counsel, than the world at other times will give them leave. (2.) Then also perhaps they may be straight going out of the world, and I may never again have any more opportunity of offering them good; and then too, probably, they may be more sensible of the reality of those things which concern another world, when they see nothing in this world will do them good, or keep them here. And when I come to any, never to omit the mention of death, which will neither stay our leisure, nor be hastened by talking of it. And herein to regard the good of a soul, rather than the pleasing of any one's fancy.

7. I desire *in all things men should rather be pleased with what I must do, than for me to do any thing meerly to please men,* unlesse in things otherwise indifferent every way, and in them indeed to be willing to please all men in all things; taking counsel, in things of that sort, of men's infirmities;

\* See note *h.* at end. G.

but in substantials onely of God's Word ; except that even in such men's weaknesse or waywardnesse may sometimes so vary the case, as that one while they may necessitate a present enforcement of a doctrine, and another time the forbearance for that season. And because the forbearance of this is ofttimes a great businesse of importance, I may bend all the strength of my prayers and wits about it ; and where I can, call also for the help of other men, more experienced in the divine mystery of gaining and feeding souls, being ready also to lend my best help to others as well, as being all fellow-workmen in the same spiritual husbandry and building, though our lots lie in several quarters.

8. I desire ever *to have a speciall care of laying the foundation aright*, first by constant catechising of all, from very children to the eldest that will admit it ; misdoubting still the ignorance of the common sort, when I come to visit them. And however they only call for comfort, yet to be most large in urging those things, which they appear to be most defective in, as in the knowledge of sin, and the nature of repentance, and even of faith it self.

9. I desire by all just means possible *to prevent all quarrels between me and any other;* and so all prejudices, as that which would much hinder my work : and to be willing to redeem their good opinion with any thing which is my own, and that I can well spare.

10. I desire *to reserve my heat, my anger, to encounter sin;* and yet so to temper it with the meekness of wisdom, as it may appear I mean no hurt, but altogether good to the sinner, and not to be wearied either out of my zeal or meekness, either with the stupidity or fierceness of any.

11. I desire *to acquaint my self so with the tempers and spirits of every one, as I may speak most directly to their consciences*, without any decyphering of their persons ; yet not

to forbear the publick reproof of any sin, because the impudence * of any person hath made their guilt notorious.

12. I desire *to account the commandment of not suffering sin to lie upon my neighbour*, (who is my brother,) *to lie principally upon me;* and therefore if publick reproof of all, in the presence of the offender will not affect him; to reckon a wise and particular reproof in private to be a debt of love I owe him, and to defer the paiment of it no longer than till the providence of God (by some special act of giving or taking away somewhat of worth and esteem) hath made him fit to receive it. But specially not to let slip the season of sicknes or remorse for sin upon any other ground; because then he hath both more need of it, and it is like to do him most good.

13. I desire *in all places, companies, and entercourses, to remember my calling.* And not only to take heed that my example (or any one's that depends upon me) pull not down at any time, what my work is to build, or build what I am to pull down; but also to know my self authorized, whereever I come, to professe my self a projector, an architect for my heavenly Master: and therefore not onely to be ready to undertake the edification (satisfaction) of any soul that cals for my help; but likewise where I shall neither take any other man's work out of his hand; nor hinder that which is more properly mine own work; to be forward and offer my self upon the least probability of doing good.

14. I desire *to renew my commission from my great Lord and Master, every time I go about any of his work;* by supplicating his grace to go forth and along with me, to the end: and to look with contentednesse and patience of faith for my reward from him alone: even the more, rather than the lesse, when being not guilty in my self of any willing fault to disappoint it, I see not the work prosper in my hands:

\* See note *i.* at end. G.

because he proportions his reward according to our work, which is *endeavour;* not *successe*, which is *his* work : and we have wrought most hard, toiled most many times, when we have least success, the want of it greatly encreasing our toyl. Besides that for the most part it is not meerly negative, but positive, through the opposition of those we would do good to, but cannot ; and this to endure is " persecution," to which is promised a great recompence of reward : * but all only from his alone grace, who first works in us mightily, to make us do and suffer all things for Him ; and then rewards us mercifully and bountifully, through Jesus Christ. To whom therefore be all service, and thanksgiving, and glory for ever.   Amen.

* Matt. v. 10, and Heb. x. 35.    G.

FINIS.

# MEMORIALS
## OF
## Godlines & Christianity.

### PART II.

Containing
1. *The Character of a Christian in Paradoxes and seeming Contradictions.*
2. *A Proof or Character of visible Godliness.*
3. *Some general Considerations to excite to watchfulness, and to shake off spiritual drousiness.*
4. *Remedies against carefulness.*
5. *The Soul of Fasting.*

The fifth Edition corrected.

By HERBERT PALMER, B.D.
Master of *Qu. Coll.* Camb.

*LONDON*,

Printed by *A. M.* for *T. Underhill* at the Anchor in *Pauls* Church-yard, 1655.

## TO THE CHRISTIAN READER.

CHRISTIAN READER,

HERE is offered thee a second part of "Memorials of Godlinesse and Christianity:" smal indeed for bulk, but the more sutable for that to the title, and the lesse burthensome to thee. Withall I must needs say, I meant thee somewhat more: but whilest (in the midst of many imployments) I was getting it ready, a strange hand was like to have robbed me of the greatest part of this, by putting to the presse (unknown to me) an imperfect copy of the Paradoxes. This made me hasten to tender a true one;* and to content my self for the present with the addition of the other lesser pieces, which here accompany them. In which if thou findest any spiritual savour, I shall be willing to own my self thy debtor for the remainder of my thoughts of this kinde, as God upon thy prayers, (which I must continually beg) shall vouchsafe to afford leisure and assistance: only entreating thee to remember, that as I count my self the more engaged by every of these publick expressions, to a more exact walking in all the waies of godlinesse and Christianity; so wilt not thou be able to answer it to God, if

---

\* This reminds us of Bacon's complaint in the Epistle Dedicatory to the earlier editions of his Essays: "I do now like some that have an Orcharde il neighbored, that gather their fruit before it is ripe, to prevent stealing." Dr Sibbes employs like terms about his "Bruised Reed," and everywhere the "Note-takers" are denounced. G.

thou content thy self with commending any, or all of that which thou readest, and thy heart and thy life be not the better. Not notions, but affections and actions are matters of true honour and solid comfort. So I leave thee to the Lord, in whom I am ever,

Thine and the Churches

Servant together

HERBERT PALMER.*

July 25, 1645.

---

\* As stated in our Introduction, the "Paradoxes" are reprinted *verbatim et literatim et punctatim* from the original "true copy." See Appendix A for a similar exact reprint of the surreptitious edition, together with various readings from "The Remaines" of Bacon, published in 1648.     G.

# THE CHARACTER OF A CHRISTIAN IN PARADOXES AND SEEMING CONTRADICTIONS.

1. A *Christian* is one, who believes things which his reason cannot comprehend.
2. Who hopes for that which neither he, nor any man alive ever saw.
3. Who *labours* for that he knows he can never *attain*.
4. Yet in the issue, his { *Belief* appears not to have been false. *Hope* makes him not ashamed. *Labour* is not in vain. }
5. He believes Three to be One, and One to be Three; A Father not to be elder then his Son, and the Son to be equal with his Father, and one proceeding from both to be fully equall to both.
6. He believes in one *Nature* three *Persons*, and in one *Person* two *Natures*.
7. He believes a *Virgin* to have been a *Mother*, and her *Son* to be her *Maker*.
8. He believes him to be *born in time*, who was from *everlasting*, and him to be shut up in a narrow room, whom Heaven and Earth could never contain.
9. He believes him to have been a weak childe carried in armes, who is the *Almighty*, and him to have *died*, who only hath life and immortality in himself.
10. He believes the God of all Grace, to have been angry with one who never offended him; and the God that

hates all sinne, to be reconciled to himself, though sinning continually, and never making, or being able to make him satisfaction.

11. He believes the most just God to have punished a most innocent person, and to have justified himself, though a most ungodly sinner.

12. He believes himself freely pardoned, and yet that a sufficient Satisfaction is paid for him.

13. He believes himself to be precious in Gods sight, yet he loaths himself in his own sight.

14. He dares not justifie himself, even in those things wherein he knows no fault in himself: yet he believes God accepts even those services, wherein himself is able to finde many faults.

15. He praiseth God for his Justice, and fears him for his Mercies.

16. He is so ashamed, as he dares not open his mouth before God; yet comes with boldnesse to God, and asks any things he needs.

17. He is so humble as to acknowledge himself to deserve nothing but evil; yet so confident, as to believe God means him all good.

18. He is one that fears alwaies, and yet is bold as a Lion.

19. He is often sorrowfull, yet alwayes rejoycing: often complaining, yet always giving of thanks.

20. He is most lowly minded, yet the greatest aspirer; most contented, yet ever craving.

21. He bears a lofty spirit in a mean condition; and when he is aloft, thinks meanly of himself.

22. He is rich in poverty, and poor in the midst of riches.

23. He believes all the world to be his, yet dares take nothing without special leave.

24. He covenants with God for nothing, yet looks for the greatest reward.

25. He loses his life and gains by it, and even while he loses it, he saves it.

26. He lives not to himself, yet of all others is most wise for himself.

27. He denies himself often, yet no man that most pleases himself, loves himself so well.

28. He is the most reproached, and most honoured.

29. He hath the most afflictions, and the most comforts.

30. The more injury his enemies do to him, the more advantage he gets by them.

31. The more he himself forsakes of worldly things, the more he enjoys of them.

32. He is most temperate of all men, yet fares most deliciously.

33. He lends and gives most freely, yet is the greatest Usurer.

34. He is meek towards all men, yet unexorable* by men.

35. He is the best childe, brother, husband, friend, yet hates father, and mother, and wife, and brethren, &c.

36. He loves all men as himself, yet hates some men with perfect hatred.

37. He desires to have more grace then any hath in the world, yet he is truly sorry when he sees any man have less then himself.

38. He knows no man after the flesh, yet gives to all men their due respects.

39. He knows, if he please men he is not the servant of Christ; yet for Christs sake he pleases all men in all things.

40. He is a peacemaker, yet continually fighting, and an irreconcilable enemy.

* See note *j*. at end. G.

41. He believes him to be worse then an Infidel that provides not for his family, yet he himself lives and dies without care.

42. He is severe to his children, because he loves them; and being favourable to his enemies, revenges himself upon them.

43. He accounts all his inferiors his fellows, yet stands strictly upon his authority.

44. He believes the Angels to be more excellent creatures then himself, and yet counts them his servants.

45. He believes he receives many good turns by their means, yet he never praies their assistance, nor craves their prayers, nor offers them thanks, which yet he doth not disdain to do to the meanest Christian.

46. He believes himself a King, how mean soever he be, and how great soever he be, that he is not too good to be servant to the poorest Saint.

47. He is often in prison, yet alwayes at liberty, and a free-man though a servant.

48. He receives not honour from men, yet highly prizes a good name.

49. He believes God hath bidden every man that doth him any good, to do so; yet he of any man is the most thankfull to them that do ought for him.

50. He would lay down his life to save the soul of his enemy; yet will not venture upon one sin to save his life that hath saved his.

51. He swears to his own hinderance and changes not; yet knows, that his mouth cannot tie him to sin.

52. He believes Christ to have no need of anything he doth, yet makes account he relieves Christ in all his deeds of charity.

53. He knows he can do nothing of himself, yet labours to work out his own salvation.

54. He confesses he can do nothing; yet as truly professes he can do all things.

55. He knows that flesh and bloud shall not inherit the Kingdom of God: yet believes he shall go to heaven body and soul.

56. He trembles at God's Word, yet counts it sweeter to him then the honey and the honey-comb, and dearer then thousands of gold and silver.

57. He beleeves that God will never damn him; and yet he fears him for being able to cast him into hell.

58. He knows he shall not be saved by his works, and yet doth all the good works he can, and believes he shall not be saved without them.

59. He knows God's providence orders all things; yet is he so diligent in his businesse, as if he were to cut out his own fortune.

60. He believes before-hand God hath purposed what shall be; and that nothing can make him alter his purpose; yet prayes and endeavours, as if he would force God to satisfie him however.

61. He praies and labours for what he believes God means to give him, and the more assured he is, the more earnest.

62. He praies for that he knoweth he shall not obtain, and yet gives not over.

63. He praies and labours for that, which he knows he may be no less happy without.

64. He praies with all his heart not to be led into temptation, yet rejoyces when he is fallen into it.

65. He believes his prayers to be heard, even when they are denied, and gives thanks for that which he praied against.

66. He hath within him the flesh and the spirit; yet is not a double-minded man.

F

67. He is often led away captive by the law of sin, yet it never gets the dominion over him.

68. He cannot sinne, yet he can do nothing without sin.

69. He can do nothing against his will; yet he doth what he would not.

70. He wavers and doubts, and yet obtains; he is often tossed and shaken, and yet like mount *Zion*.

71. He is a Serpent and a Dove, a Lamb and a Lion, a Reed and a Cedar.

72. He is sometimes so troubled, that he thinks nothing is true in Religion; and yet if he did think so, he could not be at all troubled.

73. He thinks sometimes God hath no mercy for him, and yet resolves to die in the pursuit of it.

74. He believes like *Abraham*, in hope and against hope: and though he can never answer God's Logick, yet with the woman of *Canaan* he hopes to prevail with the Rhetorick of importunity.

75. He wrestles with God and prevails; and though yielding himself unworthy the least blessing he enjoyes already: yet, *Jacob*-like, will not let God go without a new blessing.

76. He sometimes thinks himself to have no grace at all; and yet how poor and afflicted soever he be besides, he would not change conditions with the most prosperous upon earth, that is a manifest worldling.

77. He thinks sometimes the Ordinances of God do him no good at all, and yet he would rather part with his life then be deprived of them.

78. He was born dead, and yet so, as it had been murther to have taken his life away.

79. When life was first put into him, is commonly unknown; and with some, not untill they had learned to speak, and were even grown up to the stature of a man;

and with others, not till they were ready to drop into their graves for age.

80. After he begins to live he is ever dying; and though he have an eternal life begun in him, yet he makes account he hath a death to pass through.

81. He counts self-murder a most hainous sin, yet he is continually busied in crucifying his flesh, and putting to death his earthly members.

82. He believes that his soul and body shall be as full of glory as theirs that have more, and not more full then theirs that have lesse.

83. He lives invisibly to those that see him, and those that knowe him best, doe but guesse at him; yet they sometimes see further into him, and judge more truly of him than himself doth.

84. The world did sometimes count him a Saint, when God counted him an hypocrite; and after, when the world branded him for an hypocrite, God owned him for a Saint.

85. In fine, his death makes not an end of him: his soul, which was created for his body, and is not to be perfected without his body, is more happy when it is separated from it, then it was all the while it was united to it: and his body, though torn in pieces, burnt to ashes, ground to pouder, turned into rottennesse, shall be no loser: His Advocate, his Surety, shall be his Judge; his mortal part shall become immortall; and what was sown in corruption, shall be raised in incorruption and glory; and his spirituall part, though it had a beginning, shall have no end; and himself a finite creature, shall be possessed of an infinite happinesse. *Amen.*

# A CHARACTER OF VISIBLE GODLINESS.

 GODLY man is one, who being not ignorant of the wayes and doctrine of God, lives not only without scandal, but approves and practises the general duties of Christianity, and those that are special to his condition.

More particularly:

A godly man is one that loves the Word in the power of it; and at least despises it not in the plainness of it; that comes to the Word, not to censure and cavil, but to be taught and ruled; that professes not to allow himself in any known sin, but resolves and practises self-deniall, so farre as it is made plain to him, that Christ denies his desires. He is one that loves those that seem religious and conscionable, untill they prove scandalous, and be manifestly discovered for hypocrites; and then esteems never the worse of the profession it self, and of those others whom he knows no harm by. He is unwilling to believe all of such; and though he see them faulty, doth not straight condemn them to be altogether void of sincerity. Mean time he is so far from rejoycing at their miscarriages, that even particular scandals are amongst his greatest griefs. But specially he is afraid to give any ill example himself, as knowing himself made and redeemed to no other end, than that he should live to God's glory. Therefore also, he professes and resolves to do what good he can in his place; and particularly to have his family know, and fear God, and believe in Christ. He is one that accounts sin worse than shame or loss, or any other misery: and resolves to suffer rather than offend. He esteems godlines the greatest gain, and contentment a necessary piece of godliness, and that honour, pleasure, wealth, to be sufficient to contentment, which God casts upon him, while he "first seeks his kingdom and righteousness." *

And lastly, who hath so much wisdom as to take more thought how to redeem time, than to passe it away; having somewhat setledly to do besides following his pleasures, which he uses as his recreation, and makes not his business.

* Matt. vi. 33. G.

# GENERAL CONSIDERATIONS TO EXCITE TO WATCHFULNESS, AND TO SHAKE OFF SPIRITUAL DROUSINESS.

1. THE *glorious and dreadfull majesty of God*, with whom at all times we have to do, who is "a consuming fire;"* and therefore his service, and obedience to him, is not to be slighted, but to be performed with watchfulness, reverence and godly fear.

2. *Our sins*, in number exceeding the hairs of our heads, in weight, the measure of the sand; the vileness of sin generally, and the unreasonable odiousness of one's own sins, in many respects worse than any others we know.

3. *The fearful curses and punishments due to sin* (to our sins) *on earth*, and torments inconceivable and eternal in hell.

4. *The abominablenesse of sin*, demonstrated specially in that nothing could expiate it, but the bloud and death of Christ, not only man, but God.

5. *The infinite love of God and Christ* to sinfull mankinde in those sufferings of Christ for sin.

6. *The certainty of damnation*, still, to those that carelessly despise, or wilfully abuse the grace of Christ to carnal security, or willing customary sin.

7. *The manifest expressions of Scripture*, that multitudes,

* Heb. xii. 29. G.

even of those that live within the visible Church, shall yet go to hell.

8. *The devil's unwearied malice, violence, cunning*, "going up and down like a roaring lion, seeking whom he may devour,"* unto whom they that watch not, must needs become a prey.

9. *The prodigious and desperate corruption* that is in every one's heart, ready to betray us, even to the basest lust and most horrid wickednesse.

10. *The fearfull frights of conscience*, that God may awaken us withall out of our drousie dreams.

11. *The sharp and stinging scourges* even in worldly respects, wherewith God may rouse us out of our carnal security: and must, and will, with one or other, if other means will not prevail.

12. *The wretched unthankefulness* of despising his commandments, or lazily performing any service to Him, whose mercies have been and are so abundant and free toward us, as we have found them; and yet hope for infinitely more hereafter.

13. *The watchfulnesse and diligence of worldly men*, and their heat for the devil, and their own lusts.

14. *The danger that may be to us*, not only from worldly men, alluring or opposing; but even from those who are godly, and may yet prove tempters and snares to us; and so we never walk but in the middest of snares and temptations.

15. *The certain shortness* and uncertain continuance *of our lives*, subject to a thousand casualties; and nothing to be done for God, or our selves after death.

16. *The nobleness and excellency of our immortall souls*, born to higher imployment and honour, than a brutish service of the body, or Paganish pursuing of this present world.

* 1 Pet. v. 8.   G.

17. *The certainty of the hope* whereunto they are called, who seek the kingdom of God above all other things.

18. *The infinite glory of heaven*, and eternal happiness there kept in store for them that "fight a good fight, and finish their course, and keep the faith," and " love and watch for the appearance of Christ." *

19. *The exceeding greatness of the mighty power of God*, working for and in them that believe, and live by faith.

20. *The exceeding great and precious promises of all kindes*, even for comfort in this life, to them that love God, and walk uprightly, and forsake any thing for Christ, " That all things shall work together for good to them," " and no good thing shall be withholden from them ;" and for any thing they have forsaken, " they shall receive in this world, even in the midst of persecutions, an hundred-fold more, and eternal life in the world to come." †

21. *The experience of that sweet peace of conscience, and blessed contentation, and spiritual rejoycing*, even in the midst of tribulations and persecutions, that is to be seen in many of the servants of God ; and which all profess to be certainly attainable, by those that watch and pray, and are sober, and exercise their faith and grace.

* 2 Tim. iv. 7, 8. G.
† Rom. viii. 28 ; Ps. lxxxiv. 11 ; Matt. xix. 29. G.

# A REMEDY AGAINST CAREFULNES.

### Phil. iv. 6.
*" Be carefull for nothing."*

1. CAREFULNESS forbidden, is taking over-much thought, disquieting the mind, rending the heart in pieces with doubts and fears for worldly things { good, to be { missed, lost. ill, to { befall. continue.

2. The causes are { Doting too much upon the thing or comfort in danger. Distrust of { Men. Means. God's blessing.

3. The effects are divers, and not the same in all: but it appears,—

(1.) When it provokes to use indirect means.

(2.) When the means which are used, though commonly sufficient, are not counted sufficient.

(3.) When the thoughts are chiefly upon it first and last, contrary to the express charge; Matt. vi. 33.

(4.) When it breeds interruption in holy duties { Neglected. Untowardly done.

(5.) When it hinders from enjoying natural comforts

(6.) When it makes unfit for one's calling.

(7.) When it hinders freedom of spirit, and makes unfit for civil society.

4. Hence the reasons against it are many, shewing the sinfullness of it, and directing to Remedies against it,—

(1.) *It is an idolatrous sin.* If we doted not too much on such a creature or comfort, we could not be overcareful about it. See Ps. lxxiii. 25, compared with the former part.

*The Remedy is*, to apply God's all-sufficiency, who can certainly make us happy without that creature or comfort.

(2.) *It is a Paganish sin*, an infidel's sin. If we did believe God's providence, attributes and promises, we could not be so out of quiet, Matt. vi. 33.

*The Remedy is*, to lay to heart these doctrines, as becomes a Christian.

(3.) *It is an unthankful sinne.* We deserved hell and scape that, and are promised heaven instead of it; are we not bound to referre other things to God?

*The Remedy is*, to ponder well our sins, and God's great mercy in Christ.

(4.) *It is a fruitless sin.* No man gets any thing by vexing himself, God's will shall stand.

*The Remedy is*, to weigh how great a piece of wisdom it is to make a vertue of necessity.

(5.) *It is a multiplying sin.* It endangers to make one do any thing, to secure themselves from what they fear.

*The Remedy is*, to consider the least sin worse than any evil, to a true Christian's heart.

(6.) *It is a pernicious sin.* It provokes God, often to cross us in the very thing, even for our over-carefulnes about it, disappointing hopes, or bringing fears, according to our perplexed apprehensions, besides worse mischief, if one obtain their desires.

*The Remedy is*, to consider the promises made to meeknes, and the comforts of a good conscience.

(7.) *It is a prophane sin;* hindring religious duties.

*The Remedy is*, to remember God's service the end of our life, and nothing should hinder us in it.

(8.) *It an inhumane sin.* It hurts, 1. The soul, in the forenamed neglect of duties to God. 2. The body, by hindring the enjoying of comforts.

*The Remedy is*, to love our selves wisely, and our whole selves rather than our fancy in any thing, or than any one particular thing for ourselves, how seeming necessary soever.

(9.) *It is an unsociable sin*, and inhumane in respect of others; it makes unfit for all converse, and so neglectful of friends, and even be discomforts to them.

*The Remedy is*, to consider our selves not born for our selves only: others afford us comfort, and we owe the like to them.

(10.) *It is an unnecessary sin.* We have vexation enough for each day, we need not vex our selves with thought for to-morrow.

*The Remedy is*, to consider that we may die, before that we misdoubt comes: and then, as we say, the thought is taken.

(11.) *It is a self-condemned sinne.* There are none but trust men in something or other, as great as that they are now overcarefull about, or must do God with a greater matter the eternal estate of their souls.

*The Remedy is*, to reason the like in one thing we do in another, and not to disparage God while we trust men.

(12.) *It is a sin against experience*, 1. Of the bruit and even sensless creatures, God feeds the fowls, and clothes the grass. 2. Our own, Is not the life more than meat? and the body than raiment? specially the soul than either.

*The Remedy is,* to consider God our Father, who will not be kinder to a kite than to a childe, or prefer a flower before a son, nor withhold the less (being good : and who is so mad, as to say, I would have what God sees not good?) having given the greater, Rom. viii. 32.

The Lord of earth and heaven, of grace and glory, teach us ever to love him with faith and thankfulnes, that we may enjoy all good from him through Jesus Christ. Amen.

# THE SOUL OF FASTING.*

Nehem. ix. 5, &c.

1. AN *awfull regard and reverence of the glorious Ma_jesty of the great God; with whom we have to do,* by a through-apprehension of his infinite and incomprehensible perfection, in all his attributes, and of

---

* The following is the title-page of the original edition of this little tract :—

The
Soule
of
Fasting :
or
Affections
Requisite in a Day of
Solemne Fasting and
Humiliation.
According to the Pattern. Neh. ix. 5, &c.
By H. P.
Imprimatur, *Charles Herle.*
London :
Printed by *M. Simmons* for *Thomas Underhill* at the Bible
in Wood Street.
1644.

In the British Museum copy the date is filled in "Jan. 21." Prefixed was this Epistle :

"Christian Reader,—

"From the experience that often times a little thing helps the weake, and specially the willing ; and from the desire to prevent the evil of formality in our solemne Humiliation, these few advertisements are offered

his absolute Soveraignty, as Creator, Preserver, and Ruler of us and all things in the world, v. 6.

2. *Thankefulness for all the goodness of God vouchsafed to us*, by a large apprehension of all his manifold favour; generall, to his church, to our nation; particular, to us and our friends; temporal, spiritual; illustrated marvellously by our deservings, not only of no good, but of extream ill, v. 7, &c.

3. *Sorrow for our sins, and our nation's and fore-fathers' sins*, by a deep apprehension of the cursed nature of sin in general, and vilenesse of such sins in particular; aggravated by all circumstances that may be; specially by God's mercies and chastisements, vers. 16, &c.

4. *Sense of our misery, felt and feared, all proceeding from God's hand;* from his displeasure, provoked by our sins, and impossible to be avoided, but by his favour; which is not to be presumed upon, if we continue in our sins, ver. 32, &c.

5. *Faith in the covenant*, truth, goodness, and power of God, for all times and purposes, ver. 32.

6. *A covenant renewed with God* of all observance and fidelity, specially to amend what we have acknowledged amiss in our selves, and professed sorrow for, and fear of, before God or men, or both, ver. 39, and chap. x. throughout.

to thy eye and heart. Confident that the substance of them is beyond despising, except among them who not only deny but despise all the power of godliness, I have ventured to send them out thus naked and alone. If they profit thee anything thy prayers may help to quicken to some further endeavour for thy good, him who is devoted, Thine and the Churches servant in Christ altogether." H. P.

The name " Herbert Palmer " is filled in in a contemporary hand on the title-page. G.

## DIRECTIONS ABOUT THESE.

1. IN the Word read or preached, those things are to be most carefully observed, which may quicken and confirm any of these.

2. All these are to be presented in prayer, summarily in every solemn supplication such a day, private or publick: but the enlargements may be varied, and one while more of one, and another while of another.

3. Before-hand it would be greatly helpful to have written by us: 1. Amplifications upon God's attributes. 2. Catalogues of choicer mercies. 3. Catalogues of sins. 4. Aggravations of sins.

4. The day is to be begun with those thoughts specially which relate to our selves, though taking in others also.

5. And it is not to be ended without some secret, yet solemn review of the soul's behaviour, from first to last: and an earnest labouring to fasten all the good thoughts it hath had upon it, and to re-enforce the suit to God, to settle them upon it firmly and lastingly.

The God of all wisdom and grace, teach us to practise and improve these remembrances to his glory, and our eternal good by Jesus Christ.

**FINIS.**

# MEMORIALS
## OF
## Godlines & Christianity.

PART III.

A

# DAILY DIRECTION,

*OR*,

## BRIEF RULES
for daily Conversation.

*As also*

A particular Direction for the LORDS-DAY.

---

Written by *Herbert Palmer* a little before his Death.

---

*LONDON*,
Printed by *A. M.* for *T. Underhill* at the Anchor in *Pauls* Church-yard, 1655.

## TO THE CHRISTIAN READER.

CHRISTIAN READER,

HERE is another parcell of thoughts for thee, some brief Rules for thy daily conversation. Thou wilt perhaps say they are strict, at least some of them. Rules should be so: men's lives will be loose enough for all that. But some of them (it may be thou thinkest) are not of necessity. Think again, sadly and conscientiously, between God and thine own self: and thou maist possibly be of another minde. Looking God in the face, makes some things appear to be sins, and some things to be duties; after a confident out-facing men, that it was otherwise. But suppose they are not all of necessity: yet think once more, whether there is not some wisdom in them, and an advantage, if a man can bring himself to such a temper? And if they be but so much (as some of them are offered thee, under no further notion) wilt thou deliberate, whether thou wilt strive to be so wise, or not? and whether thou wilt endeavour to have thy mind in the perfectest temper or not? I will pray for thee, through God's grace, that thou maist profit by this, and all other helps, who am still

Thine and the Churches<br>
Servant in Christ altogether,<br>
HERBERT PALMER.

## A DAILY DIRECTION.

1. AWAKE with God, and lift up thy heart to him, in thanksgiving, and petition.

2. Lose no time unnecessarily, but rise as soon as thou canst.

3. However, keep thy bed, thy heart, undefiled with wicked thoughts.

4. Let not worldly matters take up thy minde, or words, unnecessarily, at the first of the day.

5. Squander not away precious time, in being too long in dressing thy body.

6. Deferre not thy solemn prayers, upon any unwillingnesse, or sleight pretence.

7. If thou foreseest any inevitable disturbance, (as particularly abroad, in some places) pray rather than fail, in thy bed, before thou risest.

8. When thou findest any unwillingness or indisposedness to pray, consider,

### I. The Necessity of Prayer.

(1.) God's commandment.
(2.) Good is not else to be expected, either.
   1. Not the thing desired.
   2. Not the blessing.
(3.) Leave is to be asked to use benefits.

(4.) Help special wanted ; against
  1. Temptations ; dangerous to fight alone.
  2. Snares ; dangerous to travel alone.
(5.) Duties to be performed ; we of ourselves not having
  1. Any heart to them.
  2. Any skill for them.
  3. Any strength in them.

## II. THE PRIVILEDGES OF PRAYER.

(1.) Esteemed, in friends and great men.
(2.) Purchased by Christ's bloud.
(3.) No man can hinder it.
(4.) No unfitness of time or place.
(5.) To pour out our whole heart, for self and friends.
(6.) Not necessitated, to method, manner, proportion.
(7.) But speak as to a father, or friend.
(8.) Of all life, heavenly imployment, noblest exercise of soul.
(9.) Special curse, not to be heard.

## III. PROMISES OF ALL KINDES.

(1.) General and particular.
(2.) For good, and against evil.
(3.) For our selves and others.

## IV. EXPERIENCES, IN SCRIPTURE, STORY, MEMORY ; OF

(1.) Prayers answered.
(2.) Comfort by praying.
(3.) Grace answerable to praying.

9. Awaken, as much as thou canst possibly, thy spirit; that thou maist pray, with all

(1.) Reverence and apprehension of the glorious majesty, persons, attributes of the Godhead.
(2.) Faith and holy confidence in Christ thy Mediator, and in the promises general or particular.
(3.) Fervency, from a deep sense of wants, weaknesses, importance of thy suites.
(4.) Humility, by reason of sin; corruption, impotency.
(5.) Thankfulness, for mercies and promises, abundant, all-sufficient.
(6.) Charity, for others' welfare; the church, the magistrate, the minister; thy friends, those that have begged thy prayers, or have thy promise to pray for them; and for the afflicted.
(7.) Care, to put away the throng of worldly thoughts before thou beginnest, least they distract thy minde.
(8.) Watchfulnes, how thou praiest, or hast praied, never resting in the outward work done, without thou feel some inward affection and fruit of thy prayers.

10. If it be possible, let the next thing be to reade somewhat of God's Word.

11. Ever begin, and end it, with lifting up thy heart to God for his blessing, upon thy

(1.) Understanding, that thou maist see his truth and will.
(2.) Memory, that thou maist retain, what thou understandest
(3.) Affections, that thou mayest
   1. Receive the truth, in the love of it.
   2. Be careful to practice it, without delay.

12. Be not in haste, but reade to learn, that thou maist be the wiser, holier, happier, for that particular word, and reading of it, therefore think of it a while with all seriousness.

13. Usually read from the beginning of a book to the end.

14. Strive not to read much at once: yet in stories (un-

less called away necessarily) break not off, till [you have] seen some issue of it.

15. Choose to read those books and chapters most frequently, that are most easy to be understood, and most readily applied to practice; as the psalms and epistles, specially the later part of them.

16. Special difficulties, as soon as thou hast time enquire of, from books, friends, ministers especially.

17. If indispensable interruption put thee from the usual time of praier or reading, take the next free time, with all diligence and watchfulnesse.

18. However do not dine, till thou hast praied solemnly alone, longer, or shorter: and read at least some portion of Scripture every day.

19. Unless on unavoidable necessity, be not absent from family prayers.

20. Quicken thy self to like zeal and faithfulness, as if thou wert alone, and call thy self to some account, for the Word then read.

21. Having attended upon God, address thy self to the businesse of the day.

22. Allot for extraordinary business, the fittest time, and then be diligent to dispatch it.

23. Having a special calling or outward imploiment, do somwhat at it every day (if possible) or take a strict account of thy self, why not.

24. Think thou dost not well, if the bulk of thy time be not taken up in thy special calling, from one end of the year to another.

25. Thy calling consisting of divers imploiments, look that one encroach not upon the other. And prefer the most important for the time present, and for the principal end.

26. Be watchful of thy diet, that thou neither eat nor drink out of season, things hurtful, excessively; that so thou

prejudice not thy self, by what was given thee for good; and so be

    (1.) Hindered in God's services, or thy own businesses.

    (2.) Hurt, in thy minde, through temptations; in thy body by diseases, pains, present or future.

27. Let not thy mind be earnestly bent, presently before, at, or too soon after meals.

28. Yet take heed of the breaches of time, and interruptions of thy business, by meals, &c. that they put thee not too far out of the way. But have a care to return again to thy imploiments, as soon as is convenient. And particularly, if it may be, within an hour or lesse.

29. Once a day read over, and recollect in thy minde, these rules.

30. Whereever thou art, look to thy thoughts, that they be,

    (1.) Free from

        1. Wicked atheism, and denials of fundamental truths.

        2. Pride, arrogance, self-applause, though praised.

        3. Lasciviousnes, covetousnes, malice, envy, matters of provocation.

        4. Impatience, grudging, discontent.

        5. Lightnesse and vanity, froth and emptinesse.

    (2.) Filled with apprehensions, of God, Christ, eternity, thy calling, the Church; and thy own last account.

31. When thou comest into company, make account thou treadest among snares, which the devil hath set to take thee. Look to thy self first, and then to thy company.

    (1.) That thou be not the worse for them, but the better for them.

    (2.) That others be the better specially not the worse any way, by thy speech, silence, actions, forbearance.

32. Bridle thy tongue so with consideration, before thou speakest, that thou afterward wish not any thing unsaid, in reference to what may befall, temporally or spiritually.

## Memorials of Godlines and Christianity. 105

33. Take heed of

(1.) All ungodiy words.
1. Atheistical.
2. Slighting or scorning religion, devotion.
3. Taking God's name in vain in the least.
4. Swearing falsly, unnecessarily.
5. Mentioning God without reverence.
6. Making jests of Scripture phrases.
7. Using them sportingly.
8. Repeating other's oaths.

(2.) All slanderous words.
1. Untruths.
2. Truths spoken maliciously, sportingly, unnecessarily, concerning others faults or imperfections.
3. Bitter provoking jests.
4. Railing speeches, though provoked.

(3.) All scurrilous and lascivious talk, one of the worst signs of a rotten filthy heart.
(4) All kinde of lies, notwithstanding any pretence.
(5.) All idle and vain words, not profiting thy self or hearers.
(6.) All peremptory affirming news, unless infallibly assured of it.
(7.) All words of heat and anger, peremptory and provoking, in disputing, though perswaded, and even assured thou art in the right, unlesse in matters fundamental for faith or practice: yet even then, let thy passion not be unbridled; as serving to gain the hearers.
(8.) In thy promises to men (and much more in vows to God) be not overhasty till thou hast throughly weighed the possibility, and convenience, lest thou be either
1. Insnared in keeping of it.
2. Incur the blame of rash or false, in breaking it.

(9.) In any disputable question, be moderate in asserting or denying, lest an unexpected argument put thee to shame, by forcing thee to alter thy sentence, or contradiction without reason.

(10.) Boast not thyself (neither speak much) unnecessarily of any thing already done by thee, or of any ability, specially spiritual, or any future action, or undertaking.

(11.) Yet deny not the grace of God in thee, or toward thee for others, or by resolutions of faithfulness to God or men.

34. Take a time (the first free season, when thy mind is in any fitness) to pray alwayes solemnly between dinner and supper, and let nothing hinder thee in it, being at home; and neglect it not through unwillingnesse.

35. Whereever thou art, inure thy self to short, frequent and fervent ejaculations to God, both of requests and thanksgivings, which will be a blessed preservative to thy soul, and gain more blessing than thou canst imagine.*

36. Particularly neglect not this upon any sensible failing of thine, even in a sinful thought, or any unexpected accident or news of importance.

37. Give not any one (specially a stranger) power to undo thee, if he will be false.

38. Have not many friends, nor count them so, till thou hast good trial of their faithfulnesse to God (being truly religious) and of their wisdom.

39. To no friend impart another friend's secret, without leave.

40. And whenever thou tellest a secret, tell it as a secret, least they take it otherwise, and so reveal it.

41. Have now and then, that saying in thy minde (*amici sunt fures temporis,*) friends are thievs of time.

* See note *k.* at end. G.

42. Yet count the communion of saints, redeeming of time.

43. Remember that some time must be dedicated to preparation, to make way, 1. For favor in others' minds. 2. For introducing a discourse advantagiously; and that sometimes it will seem lost, through disappointment of hope; which yet is to be counted wisely and necessarily imployed, and the benefit perhaps will appear afterward.

44. Do nothing to another, which thou wouldst not have done to thee or thine.

45. Do that to another, thou wouldst have done to thy self or thine.

46. Be sure to take heed of giving any scandal by thy behavior, "better thy hand or thy eie were cut off," &c. \*

47. " Rejoyce with them that rejoyce" (after the apostle's rule) "and weep with them that weep." †

48. If they require thy company, in any of their recreations, be sure they be, 1, lawful, 2, reasonable, 3, moderate, 4, of good report, therfore forbear games of lottery, gaming for gain; lest thou, or thy company, be 1, impatient, through loss, at least inwardly, 2, want what it so lavisht, 3, break into quarrels or oaths. Remember recreation is no man's occupation.

49. Let thy company (if thou canst) be ever such as may either teach thee somewhat, or learn something of thee.

50. Be sure thou admit not any wicked or profane man to be thy familiar.

51. Let not thy presence embolden any in their sin.

52. Allot some time for meditation, and that of some divine thing.

53. Particularly, each day, think of thy last, whether thou art ready for it, which will not tarry for thee when it comes.

54. When thou hearest any worthy saying, trust not to

\* Matt. v. 29. G.    † Rom. xii. 15. G.

thy brittle memory with it, but write it down; so hast thou a double record of it.

55. Willingly let no day passe without writing some good note, of the Scripture, some meditation, &c. distinguishing the day.

56. Avoid study after supper, unless on urgent occasions, and dedicate that time to refresh thy self with the comfortable society of thy friends and acquaintance.

57. Remember to break up company in time, lest sitting up late make thee either sleep in the concluding duties, or lose time the next morning.

58. Between supper and going to bed, read again somewhat of the Word, after the former prescripts, as near as thou canst.

59. Sleep not till thou hast examined thy self in all this, and in all thy actions, the day past, to fit thee for prayer, petitioning for pardon and grace, &c. presenting thanks, as in the morning.

60. Count that day lost, wherein thou hast not done and received some good, specially spiritual.

61. Lay thy self down and sleep, as in God's arms, commending thy soul to him; and compose thy self to rest, with the thought of some promise or heavenly thing.

62. Do every thing in the name of Jesus Christ, looking for strength and assistance, in and through Him, and presenting to Him, with the Father, and the Holy Ghost, all honor and glory, obedience, love, trust, and reverence, for ever. Amen.

## PARTICULAR DIRECTIONS FOR THE LORD'S-DAY.

1. REMEMBER it before it comes, for thy self and family, that none of the sacred time be lost, through worldly business occasioned by putting it off carelessly, wilfully; or sleepiness, by too much tiring out thy spirits over night, by overwatching or overworking.

2. Count it a day of spirituall liberty, wherein thou and thine, may without interruption converse with God, and benefit your souls.

3. Unless upon true necessity, make it not shorter than other dayes, by late rising, or early going to bed.

4. Rather, as much as thy body and spirit will give leave, inlarge it, as a delightfull opportunity of good, by rising earlier, and sitting up, as long as thou canst.

5. Count the publick assemblies, the solemnest service of the day, and let no pretence, ordinarily, hinder thee or thine; from being present, from the first (continuing to the last) both morning and afternoon.

6. Let all private and family-duties tend to fit thee for, or to improve the publick.

7. Neglect not to take a through account of thy self, of every main parcel of the Word, publickly read; namely of the several parts, one by one, the several psalms and chapters, and learn somewhat from every one of them.

8. The better to do this, discourse with those that are willing to hear and answer, or such as may not refuse (as thy inferiors) concerning each of these. This will help to remember, and quicken spiritual attention, of profitable things to

be learned, above that which one would imagine. We lose much benefit of the Word, because we do not bend our minds to it.

9. As the mainest rule of wisdom, in the ordering of time this day, to the best advantage; bethink thy self overnight, or in the morning early, or both, what the present frame and temper of thy mind is, and what thou wantest, that thou maiest study for a remedy to supply; and watch what God will speak to thee in his Word, or by his minister about it, that day.

10. Pray that thou maist be attentive to what specially concerns thee, and particularly the matters so thought upon; and that without mistake, and specially without repugnance of spirit.

11. Admit not, as much as lies in thee, any unnecessary worldly discourse, no not at meals; rather then look most to it, as being the time of greatest danger ordinarily.

12. Much less begin any worldly discourse, whether among other Christians, or other persons.

13. Rather than squander away those precious hours, or even minutes upon the world or vanity, if thou canst with any convenience, retire thy self, and sit alone in thy chamber.

14. By thy good will, admit not of any worldly thoughts being alone, or silent in company.

15. But pray, read, meditate, go into good company, if any be neer: sleep were better, if any need of it, than when God and thy conscience call for thy thoughts (which are the preciousest things thou hast) to bestow them upon the world or vanity.

16. Neglect not thy usual personal devotions, but rather enlarge them.

17. Take special care to improve to the uttermost, the Word preached that day, by prayer, discourse, meditation.

18. Take heed of the least excess in thy diet, that thy soul lose not of her nourishment, by that means.

19. Yet afflict not thy body ordinarily by fasting or over-spare diet, least that also interrupt thee somewhat; besides that it sutes not so properly with a day of rejoycing, as this is.

20. Before thou go to rest, fail not to consider, what this day thou hast gained or lost, that thou maist give thanks or pray.

The God of all wisdom and peace, teach us to know His will, and practice what we know more and more to his glory, and our everlasting comfort, through Jesus Christ. Amen.

FINIS.

# APPENDIX.

## A.

"*The Paradoxes," from the surreptitious edition of "July* 24, 1645," *p.* 2, *and the various readings, &c., from " The Remaines" of Bacon,* 1648, *p.* 6.*

A[1] Christian is one that believeth[2] things his reason cannot comprehend, he hopes for that[3] which neither he nor any man alive ever saw, he laboureth[4] for that hee knoweth he shall[5] never obtain; yet in the issue his beliefe appears not to be false, his hopes[6] make[7] him not ashamed, his labour is not in vain.

He[8] believeth[9] three to be one, and one to be—(1.) be three, a Father not to be elder then his Sonne, a Sonne to be equall with his Father and one proceeding from both to be equall with both: he believing[10] three persons in one nature and two natures in one person.

Hee[11] believeth [12]a Virgin to be a mother of a Sonne and that very Sonne of hers to be her Maker: He believeth[13] him to[14] be shut up in a narrow roome whom heaven and earth could not[15] contain: He believeth[16] him to[17] be borne in time, who was and is from everlasting: He believeth him to bee a weake childe carried in armes, who is the Almighty; and him once to have died, who onely hath life and immortality in himselfe.

Hee[18] believeth[19] the God of Grace to have been angry with one that[20] never offended him, and that God that hates sin, to be reconciled to him,[21] though sinning continually, and never

* The large figures—1, 2, &c., in parentheses—denote end of a page in the original tractate: and the smaller—1, 2, &c.—refer to the various readings, &c., of "The Remaines," at the close in B.—G.

making, or being able to make him satisfaction: he believeth[22] a most just God to have punished a most just per- (2.) person, and to have justified himself though a most ungodly sinner: hee doth[23] believe[24] himselfe freely pardoned; and yet[25] sufficient satisfaction was made for him.

He[26] believeth[27] himselfe to be precious in God's sight, and yet loaths himselfe in his own, hee dares not justifie himselfe (even in those things wherein hee can finde no fault with himselfe) and yet believeth[28] God accepts him in those services wherein he is able to finde many faults.

He[29] praiseth[30] God for his justice and yet fears him for his mercie: he is so ashamed[31] that he dares not open his mouth before God, and yet he comes with boldnesse to God and askes[32] any thing he needs, he is so humble as to acknowledge himselfe to deserve nothing but evill, and yet believeth[33] God meaneth[34] him all good: he is one that feareth[35] always, and yet is as bold as a lyon: he is often sorrowful, yet always rejoyceing; many times complaining, yet always giving of thanks: he is the most lowly minded, yet the greatest aspirer,[36] most—(3.) most contented yet ever craving.

He[37] beareth[38] a lofty spirit in a mean condition, when he is ablest he thinks meanest of himselfe: he is rich in poverty,[39] and poore in the midst of riches: he believeth all the world to be his, yet he dares take nothing without[40] leave from God: he covenants with God for nothing, yet looks for a great reward.

He loseth his life and gains by it, and while[41] he loseth it he saveth it: he[42] liveth not to himself, yet of all others he is most wise for himselfe: he denyeth himselfe often yet no man loves himselfe so well as hee: he is most reproached, yet most honoured: he hath most afflictions, and most comforts, the[43] more injury his enemies doe him, the more advantages[44] he gains by them: the more he forsakes worldly things the more he enjoyeth[45] them.

He[46] is the most temperate of all men, yet fairs most deliciously, he lends and gives most freely, yet[47] is the greatest userer: he is meeke towards all men, and[48] yet is[49] inexorable (4) by men, he is the best childe, husband, friend, and[50] yet he[51] hates father and mother, brother and sister, he loves all men as himself, yet hates[52] men so[53] with a perfect hatred.

He[54] desireth[55] to have more grace then any one hath in the world, yet is truly sorrowfull, when he seeth any[56] have lesse then himselfe: hee knoweth no man after the flesh, yet he[57] giveth[58] all men their due respect;[59] he knoweth if he please man, he cannot be a[60] servant of Christ's,[61] yet for Christ's[62] sake he pleaseth all men in all things: he is a peacemaker, yet is continually[63] a fighter.

He[64] believeth[65] him to be worse then an infidell that provides not for his family, yet himselfe liveth[66] and dyeth[67] without care: he counts[68] all his superioure[69] yet stands stifly on[70] no authority: he is severe to his children because he loveth them, and by being favourable to[71] his enemies,[72] hee avengeth[73] himselfe upon them[74].

He[75] believeth[76] the Angels to bee more excellent creatures then himselfe, and yet counteth[77] them his servants: he believeth[78] he—(5.)
he receiveth[79] many good things[80] by their means, and yet[81] neither prayeth[82] for their assistance nor offers them thanks, which he doth not disdain to do to the meanest Christian.

He[83] believeth[84] himselfe to be a king, how mean soever he be; and[85] how great soever he be, yet[86] he thinketh[87] himselfe not too good to be a servant to the poorest Saint.

He[88] is often in prison yet always at liberty, hee is[89] a free man though a servant: he loveth[90] not honour among[91] men, yet highly prizeth a good name.

He[92] believeth[93] that God hath bidden every man that doth him good to doe so, he yet of any man is the most thankfull to them that doe ought for him, hee would lay down his life to save the soule of his enemy, yet will not venture on one sin, to save the life of him that[94] saved his, he[95] sweareth[96] to his own hinderance and changeth not, he[97] knoweth his oath cannot tye him to sin.

He[98] believeth[99] Christ to have no need of any—(6.)
thing he doth, yet makes[100] account that[101] he doth relieve Christ in all the[102] acts of charity: he knoweth he can doe nothing of himselfe, yet laboureth[103] to worke out his own salvation: he professeth[104] he can doe nothing, yet as truly professeth he can doe all things: he knoweth that flesh and blood cannot inherit the kingdome of God, yet believeth he shall go to heaven, both body and soule.

He[105] trembleth[106] at God's word, and yet counts it sweeter to him then the[107] honey and the honey combe, and dearer then thousands of gold and silver: he[108] believeth[109] that God will never damne[110] him and yet feareth[111] God for being able to cast him into hell: he knoweth he shall not be saved by nor for his good works, yet[112] doth all the good works he can.

He[113] knoweth God's providence[114] in all things, yet is he[115] diligent in his calling and businesse as if he were to cut out the threed of his hap,[116] he believeth[117] before hand that God purposed what he shall be, and that nothing—(7.) can[118] alter his purpose, and[119] yet prayeth[120] and endeavoureth,[121] as if he would force God to save him for ever.

He[122] prayeth[123] and laboureth[124] for that which he is confident God meaneth[125] to give, and the more assured he is the more earnest he prayeth[126] for that which[127] he knoweth[128] he never[129] shall obtain, and yet gives not over, he prayeth[130] and laboureth[131] for that, which he knoweth[132] he shall not[133] be lesse happy without: he prayeth[134] with all his heart not to be led into temptation, yet rejoyceth when he is fallen into it, he beliveth[135] his prayers are heard, even when they are denied, and giveth[136] thanks for that, which he prayeth against.

He[137] hath within[138] both flesh and spirit, and yet he is not a double-minded man, hee is often led captive by the law of sin and yet it never gets dominion over him, he cannot sin, yet can doe nothing without sin, hee doth nothing against his will, yet maintains he doth what he would not, he wavereth,[139] and doubteth, yet obtaineth[140]—(8.)

He[141] is often tossed and shaken, yet is as Mount Zion, hee is a Serpent and a Dove; a Lambe and a Lion, a Reed and a Cedar: he is sometimes so troubled that hee thinketh[142] nothing to be true in Religion, yet if he did think so he could not at all be troubled: hee thinks sometimes that God hath no mercie for him, yet resolveth[143] to die in the pursuit of it. He believeth[144] like *Abraham* against hope, and though hee cannot answer God's Logick, yet with the woman of *Canaan*, hee hopes to prevaile with the Rhetorick of importunitie.

He[145] wrestleth[146] and yet prevaileth,[147] and though yielding himselfe unworthy of the least blessing he enjoyeth,[148] yet *Jacob* like he will not let him go without a new blessing.

He sometimes thinketh[149] himself to have no grace at all, and yet how poore and afflicted soever he be besides: hee would not change conditions with the most prosperous man under heaven, that is a manifest worldling.

He[150] thinketh[151] sometimes[152] the Ordinances[153] of—(9.) God do him no good, yet he would rather part with his life, then be deprived of them, hee[154] was borne dead: yet so as it had been murther for[155] any to have taken his life away.

After he began to live he was[156] a dying, and[157] though he hath an eternall life begun in him, yet he maketh[157a] account he hath a death to passe thorough.

He[158] counts self-murther a hainous sinne, yet is ever busied in crucifying the flesh and in putting to death his earthly members.

Hee[159] believeth[160] his soule and bodie to[161] be as full of glorie, as them that have more, and no more full then theirs that have less.

He[162] liveth invisible to those that see him, and those that know him best doe but guesse at him, yet those many times, judge more truly of him then hee doth of himself, the[163] world will sometimes count[164] him a Saint, when God accounteth[165] him a Hypocrite, and afterwards when the world branded him for an Hypocrite then God owned him for a Saint—(10.)

His[166] death maketh[167] not an end of him, his soule which was put into his bodie; is not to be perfected without his bodie, yet his soule is more happy when it is separated from his bodie: then when his bodie was joyned to[168] it, and his bodie though torn in pieces burnt in ashes, ground to powder, turned to rottenness, shall be no loser.

His[169] Advocate, his Suretie shall be his Judge, his mortall[170] shall become immortall, and what was sowne in corruption, and defilement,[171] shall be raised in incorruption and glorie, and a finite creature, shall possesse an infinite happinesse, glorie[172] be to God—(11.)

---

## B.

### *Various Readings, &c.*

As stated in our Introduction there are no numbered divisions in the original surreptitious edition: but in "The Remaines" of Bacon (1648) the "Paradoxes" are classified under xxxiv heads which are noted below among the various readings, &c.

## Appendix.

1. The first head extends from "A" to "vain." 2. Believes. 3. Things. 4. Labours. 5. Can. 6. Hope. 7. Makes. 8. The second head extends from "He" to "person." 9. Believes. 10. Believes. 11. The third head extends from "Hee" to "himselfe." 12. Believes. 13. Believes. 14. Have been. 15. Never. 16. Believes. 17. Have been. 18. The fourth head extends from "Hee" to "for him." 19. Believes. 20. Have [sic.] i. e., "that have never." 21. Himself. 22. Believes the just. 23. Om. doth. 24. Believes. 25. A. 26. The fifth head extends from "He" to "faults." 27 Believes. 28. Believes. 29. The sixth head extends from "He" to "craving." 30. Praises. 31. As that. 32. Him. 33. Believes that. 34. Means. 35. Fears. 36. Inspirer. [sic.] 37. The seventh head extends from "He" to "saveth it." 38. Bears. 39. Youth [sic.] 40. Special. 41. Whilst. 42. The eighth head extends from "He" to "comforts." 43. The ninth head extends from "The" to "enjoyeth them." 44. Advantage. 45. Enjoys. 46. The tenth head extends from "He" to "hatred." 47. He. 48. Om. and. 49. Om. is. 50. Om. and. 51. Om. he. 52. Some. 53. Om. so. 54. The eleventh head extends from "He" to "fighter." 55. Desires. 56. Man. 57. Om. he. 58. Gives. 59. Respects. 60. The. 61. Christ. 62. Christ his. 63. Fighting and an irreconcileable enemy. 64. The twelfth head extends from "He" to "upon them." 65. Believes. 66. Lives. 67. Dies. 68. Accounts. 69. Inferiours. 70. Upon. 71. Unto. 72. Enemy. 73. Revengeth. 74. Him. 75. The thirteenth head extends from "He" to "Christian." 76. Believes. 77. Counts. 78. Believes. 79. That he receives. 80. Turns. 81. He. 82. Prays. 83. The fourteenth head extends from "He" to "saint." 84. Believes. 85. Om. and. 86. Om. yet. 87. Thinks. 88. The fifteenth head extends from "He" to "name." 89. Om. he is. 90. Loves. 91. Amongst. 92. The sixteenth head extends from "He" to "saved his." 93. Believes. 94. Who. 95. The seventeenth head extends from "He" to "sin." 96. Swears. 97. For "he" reads "yet." 98. The eighteenth head extends from "He" to "souls." 99. Believes. 100. Maketh. 101. Om. that. 102. His. 103. Labours. 104. Confesseth. 105. The nineteenth head extends from "He" to "silver." 106. Trembles. 107. Om. the. 108. The twentieth head extends from "He" to "he can." 109. Believes. 110. Dame [sic.] 111. Fears. 112. He. 113. The twenty-first head extends from "He" to "for ever."

## Appendix.

114. Is over. 115. So. 116. Fortunes. 117. Believes. 118. Make him to. 119. Om. and. 120. Prays. 121. Endeavours. 122. The twenty-second head extends from "He" to "against." 123. Prays. 124. Labours. 125. Means. 126. Prays. 127. Om. which. 128. Knows. 129. Shall never. 130. Prays. 131. Labours. 132. Knows. 133. Be no. 134. Prays. 135. Believes. 136. Gives. 137. The twenty-third head extends from "He" to "obtaineth." 138. Him. 139. Wavers. 140. Obtains. 141. From "He" to "Cedar" omitted: and the twenty-fourth head extends from "He is sometimes" to "importunitie." 142. Thinks. 143. Resolves. 144. Believes. 145. The twenty-fifth head extends from "He wrestleth" to "worldling." 146. Wrastles. 147. Prevails. 148. Enjoys. 149. Thinks. 150. The twenty-sixth head extends from "He" to "of them." 151. Thinks. 152. That. 153. Ordinance. 154. The twenty-seventh head extends from "He" to "dying." 155. In. 156. Ever. 157a. The twenty-eighth head extends from "And" to "thorough." 157. Makes. 158. The twenty-ninth head extends from "He" to "members:" and there is then added after "members"—"not doubting but there will come a time of glory, where he shall be esteemed precious in the sight of the great God of Heaven and Earth, appearing with boldnesse at his Throne, and asking any thing he needs, being endued with humility, by acknowledging his great crimes and offences, and that he deserveth nothing but severe punishment." 159. The thirtieth head extends from "He" to "less." 160. Believes. 161. Shall. 162. The thirty-first head extends from "He liveth" to "himself." 163. The thirty-second head extends from "The world" to "saint." 164. Account. 165. Accounted. 166. The thirty-third head extends from "His death" to "loser." 167. Makes. 168. Unto. 169. The thirty-fourth head extends from "His advocate" to "happinesse." 170. Part. 171. Om. defilement. 172. Om. glorie be to God.*

---

* With reference to these "various readings" it will be observed that they are nearly all very slight, and such as a copyist might readily substitute. Nos. 141 and 172 are noticeable omissions, inasmuch as part of the former is one of the two "expressions of Lord Bacon which Montagu adduces—viz, "he is a serpent and a dove." But you might prove Bacon was the author of the New Testament if such parallelisms are to decide: the latter, as Rénusat founds upon the "Glory be to God" the train of his criticism. [See p. 17, *ante*.] Sancroft restored it and the others in comparing "The Remaines" edition with the surreptitious one. [See p. 17. *ante*.]

## C.

*Other Writings of Herbert Palmer, B.D.*

Besides the separate tractates of Palmer ultimately collected into the "Memorials," there are the following by him :—

1. *Sabbatum Redivivum:* or, the Christian Sabbath Vindicated in a Full Discourse concerning the Sabbath, and the Lord's Day. Wherein, whatsoever hath been written of late, for, or against the Christian Sabbath, is exactly but modestly Examined : And the perpetuity of a Sabbath deduced, from grounds of Nature, and Religious Reason. By Daniel Cawdrey, and Herbert Palmer: Members Of the Assembly of Divines. Divided into Foure Parts. 1. Of the Decalogue in generall, and other Laws of God, together with the Relation of Time to Religion. 2. Of the fourth Commandement of the Decalogue in speciall. 3. Of the old Sabbath. 4. Of the Lord's Day, in particular. The First Part. London, printed by Robert White, for Thomas Underhill, and are to be sold at the Signe of the Bible in Woodstreete. 1645. 4°.

Title-page, The Licence, the Contents of the first Part, Errata, To the Christian Reader, pp. 14, [unpaged,] and pp. 368.

The "Second," "Third," and "Fourth" parts of this elaborate treatise appeared in 1652, and extend to fully 700 pages. But as Palmer was dead before their publication, I do not enter into details. Cawdrey thus refers to his former coadjutor—whose name he retains in his title-pages—in the "Epistle" prefixed to "Part 2d :"—

"I have no more to say Christian Reader, but to advertize thee of one thing wherein thou art like to suffer loss ; viz., That one of the undertakers [in margin, "The Reverend Mr Herb Palmer deceased since the publication of the former Part"] of this great Work, being gone to celebrate that Sabbatism above (whereof this Sabbath is but a shadow) hath left the whole burden of perfecting these Parts upon the shoulders of the weaker instrument. Had he but lived to put the last hand and file to the work (being an exquisite Bezaleel in this Tabernacle work) thou hadst found it moe exact and perfect than now thou art like to find it." The Rev. James Gilfillan of Stirling, in his own invaluable treatise—which only lacks a more lucid arrangement and a little more *glow* to inform its ponderous mass of materials, to vindicate to itself a far higher place than it has yet attained—" The Sabbath viewed in the Light of Reason, Revelation, and History, with Sketches of its Literature," (1862, 2d edition,) thus characterises the Sab. Red.: " In the following year there appeared one of the largest, ablest, and most satisfactory discussions which the subject ever received,"—(p. 139.)

2. *The Necessity and Encouragement of Utmost Venturing for the Churches Help:* together with the Sin, Folly, and Mischief of Self-Idolizing. Applyed by a Representation of, 1. Some of the most notorious Nationall sins endangering us. 2. The heavy weight of wrath manifested in our present Calamities. Yet withall grounds of, 3. Confidence, that our Church shall obtain Deliverance in the Issue. 4. Hopes that the present Parliament shall be still imployed in the working of it. All set forth in a Sermon preached to the Honorable House of Commons, on the day of the Monethly solemn Fast, 21 June, 1643. By Herbert Palmer, B.D., and Minister of God's Word at Ashwell in Hertfordshire. Published by Order of that House. London, Printed for Sam. Gallibrand at the Brazen Serpent in Paul's Churchyard. 1643. 4°. [Text, Esther iv. 13, 14.]

Title-page, The Epistle Dedicatory to House of Commons, pp. 4, [unpaged] and pp. 71.

3. *The Glasse of God's Providence towards His Faithful Ones.* Held forth in a Sermon preached to the two Houses of Parliament at Margarets, Westminster, Aug. 13, 1644, being an extraordinary Day of Humiliation. Wherein is discovered the great failings that the best are liable unto ; upon which God is provoked sometimes to take Vengeance. The whole is applyed specially to a more carefull observation of our late Covenant, and particularly against the ungodly Toleration pleaded for under pretence of Liberty of Conscience. By Herbert Palmer, B.D., Minister of God's Word at Ashwell in Hertfordshire : a Member of the Assembly of Divines.

London : Printed by G. M. for Th. Underhill at the Bible in Woodstreet. 1644. 4o. [Text, Psalm xcix. 8.]

Order for printing and thanks, title-page, Epistle Dedicatory to House of Peers, pp. 5 [unpaged] and pp. 66.

*⁎* This Sermon—which is impassioned as Habakkuk in its exposure of national sins—gathers to itself an additional interest

from one reference to the " Doctrine and Discipline of Divorce " of MILTON. At page 57 we have these vehement words: " If any plead conscience for the lawfulnesse of *Polygamy;* (or for divorce for other causes then Christ and His Apostles mention ; *of which a wicked booke is abroad and uncensured,* though deserving to be burnt, whose Author hath been so impudent as to set his name to it, and dedicate it to yourselves,) or for liberty to marry incestuously, will you grant a toleration for all this ?"— For Milton's reply, in his grandest and most ingeniously evading style, see his Address " To the Parliament " prefixed to his " TETRACHORDON" in MITFORD'S Works of JOHN MILTON, VoL ii., pp. 136-140, (Pickering, 1851.)—At page 139, Palmer is taunted with the " chief " authorship of " Scripture and Reason." —Cf. No. 7 of this List.

4. *A Full Answer to a Printed Paper* Entituled Foure serious Questions concerning Excommunication and Suspension from the Sacrament, &c. Wherein the severall Arguments and Texts of Scripture produced, are particularly and distinctly discussed : and the debarring of Ignorant and Scandalous persons from the Sacrament, vindicated. London : Printed by Richard Bishop. 1645. 4º. Title-page and pp. 30.

In the British Museum copy a contemporary hand has filled in on title-page " By Mr Herbert Palmer," and below " Fbre 18th.'

5. *The Duty and Honovr of Church Restorers:* Set forth in a Sermon preached to the Honourable House of Commons, Septemb. 30, 1646. [Text, Esay 58, v. 12] Being the day of the Monethly Solemne Fast, at Margarets, Westminster. By Herbert Palmer, B.D., Minister of God's Word at Ashwell in Hertfordshire, and a Member of the Assembly of Divines.

Micah 6. 8.—He hath shewed thee O man what is good, and what doth the Lord require of thee, but to do justly, and to love mercy, and to walk humbly with God.

Amos 9. 11.— In that day will I raise up the tabernacle of David that is fallen, and close up the breaches thereof, and I will raise up his ruines, and I will build it as in the dayes of old.

1 Sam. 2 30.—The Lord God of Israel saith, Them that honour me I will honour, and they that despise me shall be lightly esteemed.

London : Printed by R. W. for *Thomas Vnderhill,* at the Signe of the Bible in Woodstreete. 1646 4º, pp. 63.

6. *The Principles of the Christian Religion made Plain and Easy.*

7. *Scripture and Reason pleaded for Defensive Armes*, assisted by several others. Nos. 6 and 7 I have not seen, and cannot more particularly describe. (Cf. Brook, *sub nomine*.)

## D.
### Ralph Venning's "Paradoxes."

Our copy of this little book, as *ante*, is of the "*Third* edition," 1650. The *first* was published in 1647, [Watt, *Bib. Brit.*,] or *two years subsequent to Palmer's*. So that Herbert Palmer, not Venning, led the way. It is with not a little regret that I have to announce that neither in "Epistle Dedicatory," "Epistle to the Reader," nor in text, nor in "marginal additions," is there the slightest acknowledgment of indebtedness to Palmer—a thing inexplicable: for the most superficial perusal reveals intimate acquaintance with the earlier "Paradoxes" of our author. Thus, in the very outset, we have "Concerning God in Trinity and Unity" these—

1. "He [a Believer] beleeves that which reason cannot comprehend, yet there is reason [λόγος] enough why he should believe it.

2. "He believes one God in three persons, among whom he denies not *priority* yet grants *eternity*.

3. "He believes three persons [ὑποστάσεις *verbum et ratio et verbum est ratio fidei*] in one God, two natures in one person, and one will in three persons."

Similarly there are "Paradoxes" of the same kind concerning successively God the Father—God the Son—God the Spirit—the Attributes of God—Election—the Scriptures—Creation—Angels—Man—Sin—the Lord—Grace—the Lord's Supper and Baptism—the Resurrection—Heaven and Hell.

After these, which consist of 107 in all, there follow 127 "Miscellaneous Paradoxes Practicall or a Believer clearing Truth by *Experience*, though by *seeming* Contradictions."

I cull a few examples :—

"He cryes out 'What must I *do* to be saved?' and yet he never expects to be saved by *doing*."

"He fears to commit sin more than any man yet when 'tis committed there is no man fears it less than he."

"He grieves that ever he sinned at all, and yet blesseth God that he was once a sinner."

"He is *ashamed* that he is a sinner; and yet is not *ashamed* to confess himself a sinner."

"He knows that he is not as yet delivered from fears, and yet he believes that he is delivered from what he fears."

"He affects and strives to be the highest saint; and yet is contented to be the lowest."

"He dares not put himself to death, lest he sin, and yet he thinks he sins if he die not daily."

"He knows himself to be a king, and yet refuseth not to be any man's servant."

"He finds that which he seeks for, and yet keeps seeking when he hath found."

"He believes that no man can be born twice, and yet he believes that every saint is born again."

"He believes that no man can see God and live, yet his life is in seeing God."

"He believes that God saves men freely, and yet he believes that Christ bought salvation for them."

"There is none so much in love with peace as he, yet none maintain such a constant war."

"He fears God, and yet is not afraid of God."

"God hath commanded him to love his neighbour, and yet God requires all his heart for himself."

"He is what he was not, and is not what he was, and yet is still the same man."

These may suffice. "The Triumph of Assurance" is tinged with a fine mysticism. In 1653—the "Epistle Dedicatory" to George Hughes of Plymouth, being dated "July, 1653"—a "second Part" was issued, arranged under "Four Centuries;" the last however containing only 9 . . . These 309 aphoristic sayings, which are also called "Orthodox Paradoxes, or a Believer clearing truth by *seeming contradictions*," bear the same mint-mark, and have the same *ring*. The whole are pregnant, and not a few profound: and the only painful thing is that there should be no allusion to him whose seed-corn is herein self-evidencingly fructified into many mellow sheaves.—All Venning's books are searching, intense, instructive—but I must regard this "*theft*" as a shadow upon his memory.

## NOTES.

(*a.*) St James, " If the Lord will," &c., page 55.—Thomas Fuller furnishes an apt illustration of this: " Lord ! when in any writing I have occasion to insert these passages, ' God willing,' ' God lending me life,' &c., I observe, Lord, that I can scarce hold my hand from encircling these words in a parenthesis, as if they were not essential to the sentence, but may as well be left out as put in. Whereas indeed they are not only of the commission at large, but so of the *quorum*, that without them all the rest is nothing : wherefore hereafter I will write those words fully and fairly without any inclosure about them. Let critics censure it for bad grammar, I am sure it is good divinitie."— Personal Meditations : Good Thoughts in Bad Times, p. 15, (edn. 1649.)

(*b.*) *Pastimes*, page 59. Cf. Memoir page 28 ; also Cowley, Essay 2. Of Solitude.

(*c.*) *Amatorious*, page 59.—Milton furnishes another example of this word: " A prayer stolen word for word from the mouth of an heathen woman praying to a heathen god ; and that in no serious book, but in the vain *amatorious* poem of Sir Philip Sidney's Arcadia." Answer to *Eikon Basilike*. Richardson *sub voce* supplies others from Warton and Dr Johnson.

(*d.*) " Mutual trading in spiritual matters," page 62.—Bartholomew Ashwood has worked out this idea with rare ability and unction in his " Heavenly Trade, or the Best Merchandizing : the only way to live well in impoverishing times. 1678. 8vo."

(*e.*) *Leasurable*, page 64.—This supplies Richardson's lack of the adjective in this form = *leisurable*.

(*f.*) *Charily*, page 66.—

> " · · · · Love, be of thself so wary,
> As I not for myself, but for thee will ;
> Bearing thy heart, which I will keep so *chary*
> As tender nurse her babe from faring ill."
> SHAKESPEARE. SONNET XXII.

" *Charely* circumspect " Joye : Exposition of Daniel, c. xii. 15.

(*g.*) " He understood no other calling," page 68.—I have met in some of the old Puritans [reference mislaid] with this quaint saying, "God had but one Son, and He made *Him* a Preacher of the Gospel."

(*h.*) *Broake*, page 69.—= To "traffic" or "trade:" Cf. Richardson under "Broke."

(*i.*) *Impudence*, page 71.—

"Impudent with use of evil deeds."—3 HENRY VI. i. 4.

= shamelessness.

(*j.*) *Unexorable*, page 79.—"Impartial, self-severe, inexorable." Samson Agonistes v. 5. = not to be persuaded.

(*k.*) *Ejaculations*, page 106.—An old family-nurse of ours, a fine specimen of the trusty and godly "domestic" of the ancient times, was wont to recommend us to put as much of our "praying" into "ejaculations" as possible, on the somewhat original plea, that The Tempter "kens" (= knows) we are praying if we "gang" (= go) down on our knees, and he's then sure to plague us, but he "disna ken" (= does not know) when we "ejaculate" on our feet and at our "wark," (= work.) G.

THE END.

*Ballantyne and Company, Printers, Edinburgh.*

*Expected to be ready by January* 1865,
### (I.) MSS. OF JONATHAN EDWARDS OF AMERICA.

The Rev. ALEXANDER BALLOCH GROSART,
1st Manse, Kinross,
Editor of the Works, with Memoir, of Richard Sibbes, D.D.,
(7 vols. 8vo, Nichol's "Standard Divines,")

having in his possession various UNPUBLISHED manuscripts of the preeminent theologian and metaphysician JONATHAN EDWARDS, feels disposed partially to meet a very frequently urged request, by printing a limited private impression of them. He is not at liberty, in view of a long-intended really worthy edition of the collective works, in association with Rev. Dr Tryon Edwards, of America, if once the lamentable civil war were ended—to PUBLISH. But there is no obstacle to such private circulation of comparatively a few copies.

He proposes to include —

I. A TREATISE on GRACE; a completed manuscript, divided into chapters and sections, and carefully prepared for the press by the illustrious author.
Mr Grosart has no hesitation in affirming that this Treatise must at once take its place beside the priceless "Religious Affections," alike from its kindredly profound thinking and "savour." It extends to 119 small quarto pages, closely written.
II. Selections of Annotations from his interleaved Bible—Old and New Testament. Full of suggestions, and informed by a fine spirit. These are distinct from the "Notes" already published.
III. Specimens, *with fac-similes*, of the preparations for his ordinary Sermons. These will prove indisputably, that Edwards's name is unwarrantably adduced in defence of "reading" instead of "PREACHING" the Gospel.
IV. Letters.
V. Reprint from the original MSS. of portions of the Treatise on the "Freedom of the Will," &c., &c., shewing interesting variations.

The impression it is intended strictly to limit to 250. Copies will be furnished *in the order of application*, and duly delivered at any address in London, Edinburgh, or Glasgow, which may be given. The volume will consist of a handsome 8vo, cloth extra. The price, it is calculated. will not exceed 6s. 6d. per copy, plain, and 7s. 6d. thick toned paper; the latter limited to 50. Very few remain unsubscribed for—*none* of the 50 t. t. paper.

*In preparation :*
### (II.) UNKNOWN BOOK BY RICHARD BAXTER,
Author of "The Saint's Everlasting Rest."

"The Grand Question Resolved,—What must we do to be SAVED. Instructions for a HOLY LIFE : By the late Reverend Divine, Mr RICHARD BAXTER. Recommended to the Bookseller a few days before his Death, to be immediately printed for the good of souls. London : Printed for Tho. Parkhurst at the Bible and Three Crowns in Cheapside. 1692."

This priceless little tractate by the great Nonconformist was unknown to Calamy, and appears to have been overlooked by all Baxter's Biographers. It has all its saintly author's best characteristics—richly Scriptural, fervent to passion of entreaty, pungent, pointed, and unmistakable. Our copy was formerly in the famous collection of Dr Bliss, who deemed it apparently *unique*. It is proposed to reprint it in a limited private impression. The price will be 3s. 6d. Prefixed will be an Introduction, containing an annotated Bibliographical and Anecdotical Catalogue *from actual copies* of the numerous books and tractates of Baxter, much more full than any extant, and purged from errors.

*Ready by 25th December,*

(III.) *THE WORKS OF MICHAEL BRUCE,*
AUTHOR OF
" Ode to the Cuckoo," " Elegy in Spring," " Hymns," etc., etc.—
With Memoir, Introduction, and Notes, by the Rev. ALEXANDER BALLOCH GROSART, Kinross. 1 Vol. crown 8vo, cloth antique, 3s. 6d..

*⁎*⁎* Nearly thirty years ago (1837) the late Dr Mackelvie published the "Poems" of Bruce, fully one-half of the volume consisting of a "Life of the Author from Original Sources." The "Life" won for its right-hearted and manly author the praise and gratitude of all the leading literary authorities. Long "out of print," a New Edition of the "Poems" has been a *desideratum.* Had Dr Mackelvie's health not failed him, this, in all probability, would have been prepared by him. Now that he is gone, Mr Grosart has undertaken the "labour of love;" and while awarding the original Biography all honour and all acknowledgment when quoted or in any way used, the new Memoir and Notes will be based upon independent researches which have resulted in materials elucidatory and corrective. The text of the "Poems" will be formed upon a careful collation of the first and early editions, and in part on MSS.

†⁂† Being prepared, 200 Copies of the Edition on large paper, toned (small 4to,) *with original Photographs of the Scenes of the Memoir and Poems and fac-similes.* The price will be 10s. 6d. ; and those wishing one or more copies will be so good as send their names to Mr GROSART, or to the Publishers.

*Persons who may wish a copy or copies of either or all of these volumes, will be so good as send their names and order to* MR GROSART, *as above.*

Edinburgh : WILLIAM OLIPHANT AND CO., 7 South Bridge.

---

## BOOKS BY THE REV. A. B. GROSART, KINROSS.

1. The Prince of Light and Prince of Darkness in Conflict: or, The Temptation of Jesus. Newly Translated, Explained, Illustrated, and Applied. Crown 8vo, price 5s.
   *A new and enlarged edition in preparation.*

2. Jesus Mighty to Save, or Christ for all the World : all the World for Christ. 2nd edition, royal 18mo, 2s.
   *A new edition, with additions, in preparation.*

3. Small Sins. 3rd *edition*, with additions, royal 18mo, 1s. 6d.

4. Drowned : What if it had been me ? a Sermon preached on Sabbath, 19th June 1864, in Memorial of the Death by drowning in Lochleven, of Mr John Douglas, precentor. 3rd *edition*, crown 8vo, price 4d.

5. The Blind Beggar by the Wayside ; or, Faith, Assurance, and Hope. 42mo, 2nd edition, price 1½d. *For enclosure in letters.*

6. The Lambs All Safe : or, the Salvation of Children. 3rd edition, with considerable additions. 18mo, cloth antique, 1s.

---

London : JAMES NISBET & Co., Berners Street.
HAMILTON, ADAMS, & Co.
Edinburgh : WILLIAM OLIPHANT & Co., 7 South Bridge.

www.ingramcontent.com/pod-product-compliance
Lightning Source LLC
Chambersburg PA
CBHW021936160426
43195CB00011B/1106